HARDPRESS.NET
HOME OF HARD-TO-FIND BOOKS

Volunteers' Camp and Field Book ...
by John P. Curry

Address:
HardPress
8345 NW 66TH ST #2561
MIAMI FL 33166-2626
USA
Email: info@hardpress.net

Curr~
MA
VW

VOLUNTEERS'

Camp and Field

CONTAINING

USEFUL AND GENERAL INFORMATION ON
AND SCIENCE OF WAR, FOR THE BEN
MENTS OF THE SOLDIER.

BY

JOHN P. CURRY

NEW YORK:
D. APPLETON & CO., 443 & 445 BROADWAY.
1861.

Price, 25 Cents.

VOLUNTEERS'

CAMP AND FIELD

BOOK.

CONTAINING

USEFUL AND GENERAL INFORMATION ON THE ART
AND SCIENCE OF WAR, FOR THE LEISURE
MOMENTS OF THE SOLDIER.

BY JOHN P. CURRY.

NEW YORK:
D. APPLETON & CO., 443 & 445 BROADWAY.
1862.

TO

COLONEL ROD MATHESON,

OF CALIFORNIA,

AND OTHER OF MY FORMER COMPATRIOTS IN ARMS,

ATTACHED TO THE

NEW YORK VOLUNTEERS,

𝕿𝖍𝖎𝖘 𝕷𝖎𝖙𝖙𝖑𝖊 𝖁𝖔𝖑𝖚𝖒𝖊

IS

RESPECTFULLY INSCRIBED.

NEW YORK, *May*, 1861.

INTRODUCTORY.

THE following pages, devoted to the art and science of war in camp and field, were written more for private instruction for the use of the members of several of the volunteer regiments now preparing for active service, than with any view at the outset for general publicity and circulation. The object of the writer was to give such hints and suggestions from his own experience in campaigning and camping out, as would contribute to the stock of information of those immediately under the command of friends who have had but little time to devote to the acquisition of military knowledge and few opportunities for practice on the subjects of which it treats. In so doing, he has endeavored to furnish the inexperienced volunteer, officer as well as private, with a concise yet comprehensive handbook on every matter of interest connected with the employment of troops, in camp or on the field of action, whether in offensive or defensive operations; and such hints and suggestions that might not readily occur to them for alleviating much of the hardships and risks incidental to the profession of arms. Among the subjects touched upon in this little volume, will be found useful remarks on field fortifications, instructions on artillery practice and heavy ordnance, descriptive summary of explosive substances, cavalry movements, skirmishers and skirmishing, deployments, reconnoissances, outposts, surprises, and method of attack and defence. There will also be found ample suggestions on the art of firing at long and short range, protecting the body under close fire, cross-firing, details of duty, storming parties, order of battles, strategic movements and night attacks, manner of constructing rifle-pits and temporary barricades, together with an illustration of facing, marching, and wheeling movements, proper formation of the company and regiment, and the elementary principles of the manual of arms; to which are added, the order of encampments and a most useful compendium of camp-cooking, making earth ovens, and the treatment of wounds, poison, &c., &c.

Part First.

FIELD FORTIFICATIONS AND INTRENCHED POSITIONS.—ATTACK AND DEFENCE.

FIELD FORTIFICATIONS.

THE term field fortifications applies to such works of a temporary nature, that are constructed of earth, wood, bags of sand, etc., which may be erected during the operations of a campaign, to enable an armed force to resist with confidence and advantage the attack of one superior in numbers, discipline, or equipments. Permanent fortifications are those of a more permanent and durable character. Our sea-coast defences, built of brick or granite, and massive in their construction, come under that head, as are any positions, in fact, to be permanently occupied as military works. The meaning of the word intrenchment, or lines of intrenchments, signifies field works resorted to for the purpose of strengthening the position of an army, or detachment to be employed and occupied in defending the approaches to a stationary camp, or city, or to impede the progress of an invading enemy from penetrating within the line of defence or basis of operations. If woods, rivers, mountains, precipices, and rolling ground present themselves to the eye of an engineer intrusted with the erection of intrenchments, they are natural obstacles, which may be strengthened by military art, and are always considered in the plans to be adopted and marked out for the line of defence.

Intrenchments are hastily thrown up of such perishable materials as earth, wood, etc., afford. The chief object in laying them out is to enable the assailed to meet the enemy with success, by first compelling him to approach under every disadvantage of position, and then, when he is cut up by the fire of the works, and is exhausted by his efforts to carry them by vigorous assaults, with storming parties, to assume the offensive and drive him back at the point of the bayonet. This object can only be attained by defending the works to the last extremity ; and, unless successful, intrenchments would serve no other purpose than to shelter the assailed from the enemy's fire, without probably accomplishing a single military result.

The damage received by the enemy making the assault, from the fire of troops intrenched, who do not intend to make a vigorous defence, but can see safety only in retreat, would be necessarily trifling. But in encountering the courageous efforts of the defenders to hold their position, and repel the assault, the case would be far different, and the loss greater on the part of the assailants.

This principle leads to the rejection of all advanced works thrown up in front of the principal intrenchments, and to a succession of works one behind another, when the object is to afford retreat from the first to the last.

Such manœuvring as this only encourages the enemy, and demoralizes your own troops. If an advanced work is required for the defence of a point which cannot be defended by the principal line of intrenchments, it should have a reserve force in the immediate vicinity, and its garrison not permitted to retreat and abandon their position until it is in absolute danger of being overpowered, when it should retire in good order, under cover of the fire of the reserve. As to retreating from one line to another, one of two things must happen : either the first line must be evacuated before the enemy enters, or crosses the ditch in front of your intrenchment, in good order, that the garrison may gain their second line in safety—in which case the first line will be of little service ; or else, if the assailed wait until the assault is made on the parapet of the intrenchment before retreating, the enemy will enter pell-mell with them into the second line of defence, which will then be of no possible service.

The men engaged in the immediate defence of intrenchments might be overpowered by the repeated assaults of the enemy, unless they were supported by a reserve.

The duties of a reserve are to make sorties on the flanks of an attacking column, charge the enemy at any critical moment of disorder, and to cover the retreat of the troops, if driven from the parapet. All intrenchments should contain a reserve proportioned to their importance.

The result of innumerable actions proves that the defence with the bayonet is the surest method of repelling an enemy. A sortie made upon the flank of the enemy,

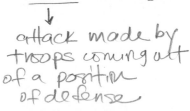

attack made by troops coming out of a position of defense

at the moment when his column is either checked by the fire of the works, or is in a state of confusion when crossing the ditch, will generally prove decisive in repelling his attack. For this reason : all intrenchments should be arranged with small outlets every fifty or one hundred yards, with a "flying bridge," to raise or throw across the ditch at such points, so as to facilitate sorties. This principle is only applicable, however, to engagements with large bodies of troops, defending works open in their rear. A small detachment should rest satisfied with repulsing the attack, and should not give up the advantage of their position, by sallying out to engage the enemy on equal terms. A retreat carries with it all the moral effects of a defeat ; it inspirits the assailants, and renders the retreating corps timid, and impairs the confidence of the troops in their own self-reliance. Add to this the confusion that must ensue among the best-disciplined troops, under such circumstances, and the importance attached to the principle will be fully justified.

To enable the troops to fight with advantage, the intrenchments should shelter them from the enemy's fire.

In delivering his fire, a soldier usually aims directly to the front, so that the line of fire and the parapet make nearly a right angle with each other.

An attack is generally opened by a fire of the enemy's artillery, whose object is to silence the fire of the intrenchments, and to drive the assailed from the parapet. When they have accomplished this result, they throw out a storming party, which is composed usually of a detachment of engineer troops, a column of attack, and a reserve, who rush forward, under cover of the fire of their artillery, to the assault. The engineer troops precede the column of attack, and remove all obstacles that obstruct its passage to the ditch. This they endeavor to fill up with bags of earth, or cross over with pieces of wood. The bayonet should be resorted to by those in the intrenchments, as soon as the enemy succeeds in crossing the ditch.

The thickness of the parapet is regulated by the material used, the kind of attack, and its probable duration.

Shot will penetrate ordinary earth, when well rammed, the distances laid down as follows:

Musket ball, one foot six inches.

Six-pound shot, three and a-half to four and a-half feet.

Nine " six and a-half to seven feet.

Twelve " eight and a-half to ten feet.

Eighteen and twenty-four pound shot—thirteen feet.

In order to insure the safety of the troops, these dimensions should be increased one-half, so that no shot shall penetrate more than two-thirds the entire distance.

The width of the ditch at the top should never be less than twelve feet. Its depth may depend upon circumstances. The earth thus thrown up makes the intrenchment or parapet, more properly speaking. The earth should be well packed, and bundles of wood, stones, &c., interspersed here and there to strengthen it and prevent the earth from crumbling. Sods with the grass upwards are excellent for covering the parapet. On the inside of all earth works, there is a slope or shelf made of earth, extending out a few feet, called the banquette, upon which the troops stand to fire over the parapet. The parapet should slope outwards, so as to enable the men to depress their pieces.

Every angle of defence should be ninety degrees, a line of defence should not exceed one hundred and sixty yards.

It should be remembered that a close fire of musketry is more deadly than one of artillery. The flanks of a line of intrenchments should be carefully guarded, or protected by a precipice, or river, or redoubts, watercourses or marshes.

A redoubt is an inclosed earth work, sometimes made square, others round, and with two or three pieces or artillery mounted in them.

A double redoubt, or star fort, is constructed as if two square redoubts crossed each other. The approaches to a line of intrenchments are frequently obstructed outside of the ditch by *trous de loup*, or pits, dug in the earth here and there, four and six feet deep, and the ground made as uneven as possible, by palisades, inundations, and mines.

Abatis works are made out of the large limbs of trees. The smaller branches are chopped off, and the ends, pointed and interlaced with care, are presented towards the enemy. Small trees with the branches facing the enemy, and fastened horizontally on the ground outside of the ditch with stakes, are excellent obstacles.

The edge of the inside of the ditch is called the scarp, and the outside the counterscarp.

Fascines and gabions are bundles of wood and large wicker-work baskets, made of willow and withes.

The gabion revetment is seldom used, except for the trenches in the attack of permanent works, where it is desirable to place the troops speedily under cover from the enemy's grape or case-shot and musketry.

An enfilading fire is to sweep your flanks with artillery or musketry.

A plunging fire is from artillery, posted on a height, or rising piece of ground.

A ricochet shot applies more particularly to a shot fired on the water at a certain angle, so that it will skip, and strike two or three times in succession. It requires a skilful artillerist to fire one on the field, in land operations. They are terribly effective when fired at an advancing column.

Cross-firing is where the fires (or shot) cross each other, and is the most effective plan to adopt in working a battery.

Rifle pits are small holes dug in the ground, large enough to admit one rifleman. They are rarely needed, except in the attack on permanent works, or a long siege. Skilful shots are placed in them to pick off the enemy's artillerists.

They are easily and speedily constructed. Say a man is six foot tall, all that it is necessary for him to do, if he wishes to shield himself in a rifle pit, is to dig a hole three and a half feet deep, and throw up the earth in front facing the enemy's position. In loose gravelly soil he can use his bayonet for this purpose.

A shirt or two, fastened at the ends and filled with sand, will oftentimes be found a good safeguard from a musket or rifle ball, by the soldier screening himself behind it, from whence he can load and fire at pleasure, without any very great risk. It should also be remembered that it is somewhat difficult to sight a person, while lying on the ground, with any degree of accuracy of aim.

Sods cut with a common knife, and turned from the earth with the bayonet, also offer a shield from a bullet.

The approaches to a position may quickly be mined by sinking, a foot under the earth, old pork or beef-barrels, filled with combustibles. In the absence of a hose or fuze to stretch underground, or magnetic wires leading to your position, by which to fire the mine, a little gulley or a dozen may be constructed from the mine to your post, charged with powder and all traces obliterated by covering with small sods.

The loss of life in battles, in the open field, is generally more bloody, though not always, than assaults of intrenched positions. The reason is, that in the former case the entire army is usually engaged, but in the latter, only the storming column. The loss of those actually occupied in the attack is always heavier, however, than the average loss of an army in the open field.

A storming column relies mostly on the bayonet for making a successful assault.

To storm an intrenched position, defended by an equal force, should never be resorted to except in case of absolute military necessity. In such an emergency, the exercise of the greatest military sagacity on the part of the officer planning the attack is required, and the most determined valor of the assaulting party absolutely requisite. The chances of success even then are more than doubtful, unless aid is rendered them by a vigorous bombardment and cannonading on the flanks of the enemy's position, sorties and efforts made to withdraw a portion, if not all, of the defenders from the point of approach of the attacking column. Every device and stratagem must be made, by feigned attacks, to enable the assaulting column to attack at the proper moment and in the weakest place. Once inside the intrenched position, reserved columns should instantly be hurried forward to their succor.

RECONNOISSANCES.

The term reconnoissance is a detailed description of any extent of country, with a view of ascertaining its resources for the movements and subsistence of troops. The importance of reliable reconnoissances for all military operations is so great that they should be thorough and complete. It consists of two parts: a map, describing the topographical features of the country, and a descriptive memoir.

The reconnoissance of an enemy's position is one of a special nature, and none but a skilful officer should be intrusted with it. He seeks information of the force of the enemy, the number of guns; and if intrenched, his exact position, the extent of ground he occupies and its character.

In troops marching, he will endeavor to obtain their number. To an unpractised eye, a column composed of five hundred men is often estimated at double the number.

Troops marching in close or open column may be computed by the average number in platoons, the distance apart, and the time occupied in passing a given point, whether by quick or double quick time. A stop watch is necessary, and the result may easily be ascertained.

RECONNOITRING PARTIES.

Reconnoitring parties, when making observations of the enemy, should observe the following precautions: to leave sentinels or small posts at intervals; to transmit intelligence to the advance posts of the army, unless the return is to be by a different route; to march with caution, beware of ambuscades, avoid fighting, and see if possible without being seen; to keep an advanced guard; to send well-mounted scouts ahead of the advanced guard, and on the flank of the party; to instruct the scouts that no two should enter a defile, or mount a hill together, but to go one at a time, while one watches to carry the news if the other is taken, and warn them.

ambush

INTRENCHED POSTS.

Unless an army be acting on the defensive, no post should be intrenched, except to cover the weak part of the lines, or at points which the enemy cannot avoid, or in mountain warfare, or to close a defile, or cover winter-quarters.

Any intrenchment that requires artillery is considered a post, and a guard or garrison, and commander assigned to it. In dark weather he redoubles his vigilance. He permits no flags of truce, deserters, or strangers to enter. If a flag ought to pass his post, he bandages his eyes that he may not observe his position. He refuses admittance to a relief or other party until he has carefully examined them. In case of an attack, he does not wait for orders, but makes the best defence he is capable of. If unsuccessful, he may spike his guns and rejoin the army under cover of night.

DEPLOYMENTS.

light infantry or calvary deployed as screen a tactical position

A company may be deployed as skirmishers, either forward or by the flank. It is deployed forward, when it is behind the line on which it is to be established; and by the flank, when already on that line. In both cases, it is divided into three platoons; the right and left platoons, denominated, respectively, First and Second platoons, form the line of skirmishers; the centre platoon, the Reserve. A line of skirmishers should, if possible, be alligned; but, to obtain this regularity, advantages which the ground may present for covering the men, ought not to be neglected.

The intervals between files of skirmishers should not exceed fifteen paces.

The captain of a company gives a general superintendence to the deployment of skirmishers, and then throws himself about seventy paces in rear of the line, taking with him the first bugler, or drummer, and two or three men from the reserve.

Skirmishers should be selected from among the best marksmen in the ranks.

They are thrown out after a line of battle is formed to open the engagement; also, on the flanks of an army in retreating or advancing, co-operating with the rear and vanguards of the same.

GUERILLA WARFARE.

This, the most barbarous and inhuman mode of warfare known, and by no means recognized among honorable combatants, is generally resorted to by irregular troops for the purpose of harassing and annoying an invading army entering an enemy's territory. They usually murder for pay and plunder, and are not prompted by any spirit of patriotism or honor. It is seldom they wear any uniform or distinguishing mark by which they may be known from peaceful persons, but assume such disguises as may best answer their purpose, such as farmers, laboring men and drovers, so that they may more readily escape detection, by throwing their arms into the nearest ditch in the event they are hard pressed. If captured with arms in their hands, they justly merit hanging by the roadside; and as no quarter or mercy is recognized by the guerilla, none should be shown him. If taken, even without arms, it is customary for them to affect the character of non-combatants, and hope by imposing upon the credulity of their captors by various pretences to be allowed to run at large again, to pursue the same murderous mode of warfare. The greatest care and precaution, however, should be adopted, and the most rigid scrutiny resorted to by the captors in detecting such rascals, so that really innocent non-combatants may not suffer for the guilty.

Guerilla warfare consists, mainly, in making night attacks, waylaying strangers, the free use of poison, incendiarism and vandalism, firing upon victims from ambush, under cover of hedges and ditches, and in robbery, pillage, and assassination.

Other infamous means are oftentimes resorted to by them, such as poisoning wells and streams on the route of march ; furnishing poisoned food to a scouting party, or an army, under the cloak of friendship and fair dealing, and in massacring the wounded left after a route on the field of battle.

If a guerilla is caught, no clemency whatever should be extended to him.

Light troops and mounted rangers are the most effective in suppressing guerilla bands ; and make excellent flankers when a column is advancing or in retreat.

FUGITIVE-WANDERINGS.

The chief fault of recruits is in firing too high; but this must not be understood that they should fire too low by any means. Only at point-blank range should the piece be aimed directly at the object. If beyond that distance, the muzzle of the piece should be slightly elevated, so as to allow for the falling of the ball by its own weight. In a long flight this always occurs.

As an illustration : say, at one thousand yards' distance you wish to hit an adversary in the breast, you must aim for his head; and again, if the distance off is still greater than that, you must aim a little higher. Care, however, must be taken to make a *line* shot of it, and not aim to the right or left of the object, but directly over it. If a strong wind is blowing from the *left* of you, aim a little to the *right* of your object ; as, if you aimed directly at it, the force of the wind would carry your ball out of range. If the wind is blowing on your right side, then fire to the left of the object aimed at.

When firing, the least motion of your arms or body should be carefully avoided, as the slightest movement on the instant of pulling trigger will destroy the aim, and throw the ball out of line.

Inside of point-blank range, the muzzle of the piece should *fall half an inch below the right eye*—that is, if your adversary stands on as level a piece of ground as yourself. If not, then aim directly at the centre of his breast.

Cross-firing is the most destructive. When a regiment is drawn up in line of battle, preparing for action, a piece of artillery posted at each flank can be made immensely serviceable in either attack or defence. If a column of the enemy approach, the pieces on the right and left flank should converge their fire directly on the front centre of the enemy's column, while those in the ranks fire direct. By thinning out his centre, his flanks must fall in to fill up the vacuum. A regiment should also be instructed in forming V's and W's, when a terrible cross-fire may be obtained by those on the left flank firing left oblique, and those stationed on the right, to the right oblique, while the artillery stationed at the *pivot* fires direct. It is almost impossible to penetrate this fire.

USEFUL HINTS AND EXPERIENCES.

There should be for every 100 men, as useful articles of camp furniture, ten camp kettles, in nests of five, to hold not less than four gallons, and made of Russia iron; also, ten mess pans, of same capacity. Each man should have one tin plate, tin cup, knife, fork, and spoon, bearing his own mark. One cook and two assistants are enough for a company, where bread or biscuit is supplied. They make the coffee, bean soup, and cook the meat. Yeast powders should be furnished by the company commander, as it is not an article of the ration. Sugar and coffee rations have been increased by the army since the old regulations. Six tents for 100 men are enough, where the Sibley tent is used; one for every five men of the common army tent. Each man should have one heavy " four-point " blanket, which will answer for two on a march. Every man should have one light navy-flannel sack-coat, and pegged shoes, wide, well nailed, and large; three pair cotton socks, and each a soft felt hat, of a dark color —dark drab is preferable. Light or red caps should never be worn in action, for they offer a sure mark for an expert corps of riflemen. In a night attack on the enemy, or to effect a surprise, dark colors alone should be worn. When on such expeditions, some precaution must be observed not to expose burnished arms to the reflection of a light, or, if it can be avoided, even to the moon's rays. The best plan is to carry your arms reversed. Keep clear of the main roads, and take to the fields, or side trails, as you approach your point of surprise and attack. Move along the sides of hills, instead of crossing on top, and follow in the shade of trees when the moon is shining, and do not expose yourselves with the horizon in your rear, so that your forms may loom out distinctly against it—for sentinels are supposed to be, in time of war, ever on the alert.

Each man should also provide himself with a piece of castile soap, a hole in the centre of it, and a cord passed through, and fastened by a slip knot; also a short coarse comb, toothbrush, and coarse towel, eighteen by twelve inches in size.

Wash the body at least twice a week, and the face, chest, and arms daily.

If in camp, exercise daily by running, jumping, football, or shinty.

Keep the bowels free, and avoid eating oily meats, fat, or drinking an excess of coffee. The mind and body both become dull and sluggish by too much indulgence in the latter.

When overheated and exposed to the sun, you may cool off by sopping the wrists with cold water and immersing the arms to the elbow. This cools the arteries of the arms, carrying the blood to the heart, and a few seconds after, the entire body feels refreshed. Take but a mouthful of water every few seconds, if you wish to quench your thirst. When overheated, drink then by what we may call sipping it carefully, lest you produce too sudden a reaction in the system, and endanger your life.

The head may be protected from the heat of the sun. when on a march, by laying a small piece of wet sponge directly over the crown, and keeping the head covered with your hat or cap.

If you have no sponge, your towel folded and wet, or some wet leaves, will answer the same purpose.

To protect the eyes, when marching over a sandy country especially, stick small twigs of leaves under the front of the cap; besides shading the eyes, the color of the leaves will neutralize the peculiar hot glare from the sand, which very often produces blindness.

When firing at an enemy, the eyes should always be carefully shaded.

Provide yourself also with an india-rubber slip to lie on.

TO MAKE A TENT COMFORTABLE.

The best position for a tent to be pitched, is on sloping ground; the opening facing the slope. If it is a single tent, without a "fly," the top may be covered with small branches of trees, attached to the tent pole. When you see a rain storm coming on, wet your tent and spread the water over the surface with your hands. This prevents the rain from striking through. Intrench your tent by
2

turning up the sod all around it, and plastering the interstices between the sod with mud. It should be about
eight inches high. If you wish to raise the interior of
your tent a foot higher than the outside ground, sod it
with sods. If you desire to keep it dry and warm, dig a
hole in the centre a foot deep, with a small gully or ditch
from one side of it, extending to the outside of the tent.
Build a fire in the hole, and cover it and the gully with
sod carefully fitted in: cut a small vent in the sod, covering the hole and another at the extreme end of the gully
on the outside. These will create a draft, the vent outside carry off the smoke, the fire kept burning slowly,
and the interior of the tent kept perfectly dry and com-
fortable.

TO MAKE AN EARTH OVEN.

This is made entirely of sod, build up around an oblong
trench in the ground in which the fire is built. Pieces
of hoop iron, or iron rammers, are placed over the trench
to rest the bread, meat, and stews to be baked or cooked.
The sides and top of the oven should be carefully covered, the sod on top fastened in their place by pieces of
wood imbedded in them, and the interstices carefully
closed with mud, mixed with straw or grass. A chimney
about a foot high may also be constructed of sod; and a
small vent, dug into the trench in front under the bars of
iron, will afford sufficient draft for cooking purposes. The
door leading to the oven, may either be a sod, or made
as suits the pleasure of the soldier.

The whole can be constructed in fifteen minutes.

FULMINATING CAP POWDER.

Eight and a half parts of powder, fired with percussion caps, are quite equal in force to ten parts of gunpowder, fired in the ordinary way by means of pan and flint.

CONFINED AIR.

Air in the immediate juxtaposition of combustible material creates terrific force when fired, and is likely to explode the piece. Always be careful then that your cartridge is rammed well home, before discharging your piece.

TO PROTECT THE BODY UNDER CLOSE FIRE.

When required to come under close fire, the body may partially be protected in front from the chin to the thighs, by folding your blanket in five or six thicknesses, and fastening it under your cross-belts and waist-belt, leaving the end hanging over your stomach. If the blanket is wet, it affords more resistance.

TO MAKE AN AMERICAN FLAG.

The breadth to be three-fifths of the length. Thirteen stripes of equal width, seven red, six white. The union of blue two-fifths of the length of the flag and seven-thirteenths of the breadth.

I. e.—A flag 15 feet long should be 9 feet broad. The union should be 6 feet long, by 4 feet 8 inches wide, and each stripe about 8 inches wide—the upper and lower stripes are *red*.

The stars in the field can be arranged to suit the pleasure of the maker. The best way is in lines, one star below another. The stars arranged into a large star are not according to army or navy regulation.

Part Second.

ARTILLERY AND ARTILLERY PRACTICE.—MUNI-
TIONS OF WAR AND EXPLOSIVE SUBSTANCES.

ARTILLERY AND ARTILLERY PRACTICE.

THE wonderful improvements made in heavy ordnance and field artillery, within the past thirty years, have caused almost a complete and radical revolution in the old established system of warfare. The six, nine, twelve, eighteen, and twenty-four pound carronades, together with the long twelve and eighteen-pounders that were once considered such formidable weapons, are now spoken of by artillerists with feelings of unmitigated contempt when contrasted with eight, ten, and thirteen-inch chamber guns, rifled cannon, and the modern howitzer. But a few years since it seems when all our forts and defensive positions, as well as our men-of-war, were armed with the former guns. Nor were we alone in this position, for all the nations of Europe were similarly situated. To boast of a battery of twenty-four pound carronades, with a few long eighteens, on the decks of an old-fashioned line-of-battle ship, or defiantly peering out from the casemates of one of our fortresses, was to consider ourselves well guaranteed for offensive and defensive demonstrations, whenever it became necessary to uphold the dignity of the flag and maintain ourselves among the nations of the earth as a first-class military power—ready at all times to display our strength when occasion required.   All our naval battles were fought with this calibre of guns, and yet we hear complaints that our ships carried heavier mettle in several of the actions afloat when we were pitted against the enemy than they did, although, as far as the number of pieces worked in battery on either side were concerned, in many of our naval engagements, they were nearly if not quite equal.   They urged, in extenuation of the loss on their part, that we threw a heavier weight of mettle at each broadside than the calibre of their guns would admit, though on several occasions our forces had a less number of guns in action than they themselves.   This only goes to show that, in our early history as a nation, England and France were no better off in this respect than we were.   They had not then arrived at that perfection in inventing and constructing those terrible engines of destruction, for which they are now so famous.   During the Revolution, and in the war of 1812, no heavier mettle than six, four, and nine-pounders were used in land operations, except in sieges, when eighteen and twenty-four pounders were the largest cannon brought into requisition. The former came under the classification of light artillery, used on the field; and the latter, siege guns.

By what is known as chamber guns, one of the modern

improvements in ordnance, is that the piece is larger in the interior space at the breech than at the bore. This space gives greater force to the explosion of the powder when it is fired, and of course must project the ball to further distance and with more velocity than the old models. They may be used to advantage in throwing shells, besides grape, shrapnel, canister, and round and double-headed shot. In throwing shells, greater accuracy of aim and length of range are obtained than with the common mortar.

All fire-arms of large calibre come under the general term of artillery. The term ordnance applies mostly to heavy guns; but, at the same time, all guns in our service come under the general appellation of ordnance, whether light or heavy. The latter are commonly manufactured of iron, some cast, wrought; and others out of what is known as gun metal, composed of tin, iron and copper well fused, though other metals are oftentimes used in connection with iron and tin for the same purpose. Wrought-iron guns are far superior to cast-iron ones, for the reason that they have fewer flaws in them than the latter description, and are certainly less liable to burst than the others. Large wrought-iron guns, however, should be welded in pieces, and only a small amount of heat employed.

Rifled cannon and howitzers—as light artillery—are manufactured more frequently out of steel and brass, though some are made out of the composition above mentioned.

[handwritten: Small canon on wheels]

HOWITZERS.

A howitzer is also a chambered gun, used principally for throwing shells, grape, and canister. They are of three kinds: the mountain howitzer, for carrying over rugged countries, lashed to mules, if necessary, and is quite light and short in pattern; the field and boat howitzer, of medium size, and the heavy, long sea-coast howitzer, for permanent works. The mountain howitzer carries usually six-pound projectiles; and occasionally we find one carrying twelve pounds. The former, being lighter, are preferable for mountain warfare. The field and boat howitzers are usually twelve-pounders. The sea-coast howitzer carries much heavier weight of metal, and is particularly adapted for hurling shells.

[handwritten: explosive shells]

PAIXAN GUNS.

[handwritten: looks like canon]

The Paixan gun is entirely a French invention, named after its originator, who was a general in the French army in 1822. He was the first person to bring into use shell guns, after which they were adopted by the American Government; the old carronades done away with for active service; the long twelve, eighteen, and twenty-four pounders cast aside, and our men of war and sea-board forts armed with medium-sized and long thirty-twos and forty-twos of the Paixan make.

They are chamber guns, and continue to be in very general use.

To make ourselves better understood, we would mention that the range of a medium-sized gun is not so great as a long piece.

COLUMBIADS. Cannon

The modern columbiad is nothing more than a slight improvement on the Paixan gun. They are much larger however, heavier, and longer, and carry eight, ten, and eleven-inch projectiles, which means that the shot or shell is of the same width as the diameter of the bore of the gun. It is usual, moreover, in speaking of very large ordnance, instead of saying sixty-eight, ninety-two, and one hundred and twenty pounders, to refer to them as so many inch guns, whatever the diameter of the bore or muzzle may be.

The columbiad is a most formidable weapon when properly handled by experienced artillerists, and will carry heavier solid shot at longer reach than the ordinary Paixan, and still more so than that of the sea-coast howitzer.

DAHLGREN GUNS. Cannon

The Dahlgren gun is named after Captain Dahlgren, United States Navy, its inventor, and a gentleman who may very properly be considered one of the few most experienced gunners in either branch of the service. His thorough knowledge of the power and force of various explosive substances, and of ordnance, on which duty for many years he has been assigned, with great credit to himself and honor to the Government, places him in the front rank of our most distinguished officers. After undergoing a variety of dangerous experiments, in which his life was constantly in jeopardy, and with the exercise of considerable ingenuity and skill, he succeeded in perfecting his design so well that he produced a gun which many men of military experience consider far superior to any large ordnance yet introduced to the notice of the general public.

The peculiarity of the construction of the Dahlgren gun is such that the danger of its bursting, except by an excessive overcharge, is almost a matter of impossibility, while the effectiveness and range of its fire are quite equal to the best of other patterns, without their objections.

As all guns burst at or near the breech, this one is made of enormous thickness at that part to what other cannon are, and gradually tapers smoothly down to the muzzle. The middle of the piece, which offers the least resistance to the explosion of a charge, is not so thick as the muzzle, however, where in most other ordnance it is liable to crack open in slight seams after repeated discharges.

They are also chambered guns, most of them of nine, ten, and eleven-inch bore, though we are under the impression several of still larger calibre have been constructed after the very same model.

They are enormously heavy, but are mounted in such a simple and durable manner that they may be elevated or depressed, shifted to the right or left, with as much ease and facility as an ordinary cannon. They will throw eleven-inch shells to the distance of four miles, and, what is known among skilful artillerists as an eccentric movement, an additional half mile further might possibly be obtained. They are powerful weapons to cope against, even with large sized rifle cannon, and can be worked to great advantage either in battery or afloat.

MORTARS, SHELLS, AND TORPEDOES.

Mortars are in shape almost like a bell, and are set in what is called a mortar-bed. They are principally used for throwing shells, but are heavy and unwieldy for manœuvring, and their precision of aim is not so reliable as in chamber guns. They have been in use several centuries, but have acquired such terrific destructiveness from modern improvements in projectiles, that they spread death and havoc whenever brought to bear against a city. At one time they were made serviceable on board small vessels, specially constructed to receive them, and denominated "bomb-ketches," for assisting in the shelling of fortified cities and sea-coast defences; but, since the modern improvements in gunnery, will soon go out of practical use.

Shells used in both mortars and chamber guns, are hollow-shot filled with various explosive materials, with a small brass screw at one end, through which projects a fuze. This fuze connects with the inside of the shell, and is made of various sizes. Some of them will burn half a second, others one, two, three, four, or five seconds, depending altogether on the time you wish it to burn.

8

The fuze ignites the instant the shell is fired from the gun or mortar, and when burned out explodes the shell. By a little practice an artillerist can soon get the exact range he wishes to hurl the missile at. If the object cannot be reached in two seconds, and it requires four or five seconds for the shell to reach it before it will explode, then insert a four or five-second fuze. If you desire it to explode in two and a half seconds, then insert a two and a half-second fuze. The exact time the shell will require to reach the object may easily be reckoned by a stop-watch. Time the flight of one of the shells aimed at the spot, from the instant the gun, or mortar is fired until you see it fall at or within the place. If it is three seconds, then you require a three-second fuze for every shell fired at the same object thereafter.

Shells were formerly called bombs, and hence the word bombardment. Now, however, when they are used against a place, we call it shelling the city, or fortress, as the case may be.

A shell fired from a mortar describes a parabola through the air before it strikes, and if you are on the look-out you may avoid it. When it falls near your presence, drop suddenly at full length on the ground until after it explodes. It will explode upwards when it strikes, and outwards at an angle of several degrees.

Shells fired from a gun, unless they are thrown from a long distance, when the piece must necessarily be elevated, are not so easily avoided. If you are near a shell while the fuze is burning, lay down, and throw dirt, sand or water, or piece of cloth at the fuze to put it out, before it explodes the powder.

Many mortars are made of stone, but the most of them are of iron. The largest in our service will throw 13 and 15-inch shells.

There are far more powerful explosive substances than powder, frequently used for charging shells, one of which is fulminate of mercury. When charged with the latter ingredient no fuze is required, as the fulminate would explode the shell by its own concussion. It is exceedingly dangerous to handle, however, the accidental dropping of a shell filled with this substance from the hands, say only a distance of four or five feet, would explode it. Shells may be charged with some degree of safety by admitting one-fourth of fulminating powder of mercury, to three-fourths of common powder. Torpedoes six inches long by three wide, made of tin, and filled with fulminating powder and a three or four-second fuze inserted, can be made terribly effective in blowing up brick walls. In a march through an enemy's city, where an incessant firing is maintained from the windows and housetops along the route of march, loosen a brick or two from the front of the wall, a few feet from the ground, insert one or two of these torpedoes, light the fuze, and get out of the way. These would be sufficiently powerful to topple the front of the structure at least to the ground, and expose those inside to instant destruction by the falling of the roof and timbers. Fulminate may also be used in charging hand grenades, but every care and attention must be observed in handling them when so loaded.   There are several other far more dangerous explosive substances than either powder or fulminate, so terrible indeed in their nature that the public mind would stand appalled were they known and used in warfare.   They may be specially used for charging shells, grenades, or torpedoes, but as a matter of policy we refrain from mentioning them.

Percussion powder, of which caps are charged, contains about one-half of fulminate to one-half of common powder, mixed to a consistent paste with water.

Asphyxiating shells, when thrown into a fortress, impregnate the air with a poisonous substance, which, if sufficient in density, would paralyze, if not destroy, the life of every one breathing the atmosphere in close proximity.   The shells are charged with a chemical preparation, of which *cyanuret of potassium* is the principal agent.

With rifled cannon, throwing conical-shaped projectiles instead of round ones, shells may be made with two or three chambers, according to the length of the bolt-shaped projectile, and be made to explode the second and even the third time after the first explosion.

RIFLED CANNON.

Decidedly the most effective of modern weapons, more especially for light artillery practice, is the James' celebrated steel rifled cannon.   The result of numerous experiments made by the English Government with this engine of war, is the great range of its fire, precision in which its projectiles reach their mark, and capacity for discharging conical balls and shell. There can be no question about its being far ahead of any other light artillery now in use. It has been demonstrated that it can shell dense masses of troops in column, using the old brass six and twelve-pounders and howitzers, stationed at a distance of two or three miles, with ease and accuracy of aim, while the discharges of the latter would fall far short in silencing them. No artillery company that is preparing for active service should be without them. It is a simple matter, however, to rifle the old-fashioned brass guns used by some of our companies; but none but an expert should be permitted to complete the job, as there is no little danger, if the rifling or groove is turned too much, the piece may explode at the very first discharge. This would be occasioned by the resistance of the rifling or groove to the flight of the projectile from its bore. The old-fashioned pieces which may be rifled should only have enough turn to destroy the *windage*, and that would be sufficient for all practical purposes. If too much rifling is allowed, it does not increase their efficiency or range. As long as it is barely enough, as we remarked before, to overcome the windage, and give the necessary rotary motion to the projectile, is all that is required. For very heavy rifled guns of large calibre, we have our doubts about their being superior to the Dahlgren gun. They may send their missiles with far more certainty of hitting the object aimed at; but we scarcely believe to any greater distance than the former. The larger the rifled gun, the greater is its expansion,

when, like all other cannon, it becomes overheated after
a succession of discharges. Were this continued, even
with a reduced charge of powder, the resistance caused
by the very rifling to the escape of the projectile is more
apt to burst the piece and destroy the lives of the gunners,
than guns of as large calibre that are not rifled. Again,
a rifled cannon also becomes heated quicker than an
ordinary gun. This is a very serious objection in time
of active firing; and while waiting for a gun to cool off,
the battle might be lost, unless there were reserved guns
ready at hand to take their place in position.

The Armstrong gun is a rifled cannon, also of English
invention. It is reported to have a range of five miles;
but in other respects the only difference between this
one and those we have mentioned, is that it is loaded at
the breech.

To our volunteer artillery companies preparing for
an active campaign, we would suggest that, if they have
not the improved English rifled cannon, to get their brass
pieces slightly rifled; and also, in preparing ammunition
for the charge, to provide themselves with a few conical-
shaped shells, incased with a thin sheeting of lead, and
filled with two-thirds (or more, on experiment) of fulminating powder, to one of common powder. They require no fuze to ignite them, but will explode like a
common torpedo the instant they strike, tearing to pieces
every thing within reach. After a gun becomes heated,
water should be poured copiously over it, and the sponge
made quite wet when sponging the piece. The charge
should be immediately reduced to the second; and, after

a few more rounds are fired, if the piece continues to grow hotter, come down to the third charge, and fire less frequently, until it cools off.

Projectiles for rifled cannon are mostly made in the same shape, only on a larger scale as the Minié rifle ball, pointed at one end and with a slight inverted or concave base. It is necessary that they should either be of lead, or iron incased in lead. The explosion of the cartridge swells the base of the projectile, so that it fits the groove or screw, sending it forth on its mission with unerring velocity and destructiveness.

All cartridges for cannon, howitzers, or mortars should be put up in flannel bags of sufficient size only to hold the actual amount required for the charge. Various colors of flannel bags, such as white, red and blue, may be used: the first denoting that they contain the first charge, the others, the second and third.

Great care should be observed in loading that the vent is closely covered when the sponge is inserted. After being inserted, it should be turned but once, and then withdrawn. If the vent at the time of sponging is not well stopped, premature explosion is likely to follow the instant the cartridge is rammed home.

Coarse-grained powder is used for cannon; with fine rifle powder the piece is liable to hang fire.

In priming, see that the priming wire sufficiently pricks the cartridge, and that the tube or fuze is pushed home.

In loading, it should be recollected that only one inch of confined air between the cartridge and the projectile, will endanger the bursting of the gun the instant it is fired.   Confined air, when fired in contact with powder, explodes with terrific force.

To avoid accidents, arising from this evil source, see that the projectile is rammed compactly against the cartridge. This may be accurately determined by the length of the rammer, inserted when the piece is not loaded and when it is, and mark on one end of the rammer the difference by a notch.

OF THE PIECE.

The right and left of the piece, as relates to the station of the men, is determined by the position of the man placed in rear of the gun and looking towards the muzzle. The reverse is the case with the limber, the right and left of which are always determined by the right and left of the driver.

The squad for the service of a field piece, is formed in two ranks, in close order, from right to left, as follows: Chief of the piece, covered by the non-commissioned officer; No. 5 man, covered by No. 6; the gunner of the right, covered by the gunner of the left; No. 3 covered by No. 4, and No. 1 covered by No. 2.

We give the position of the squad above, that inexperienced persons may see how they are placed, and omit all the detailed manœuvres of the gun, as they would occupy more space than we have to spare, our desire being to make our remarks as general as possible. Six pieces, each with its caisson, are here supposed to constitute a battery. The pieces may be six or twelve-

TWO WHEELED CART

SIX "GUNS" = BATTERY

pounders, or even heavier, or they may be mixed. The pieces and caissons are numbered from right to left. Each chief. in giving the command for a movement, designates his piece by its number. The battery is divided into two sections, each section consisting of two pieces, with their caissons, numbered from right to left.

In advancing, each piece precedes its caisson. In retreat, each caisson precedes its piece.

For manœuvring, the battery is formed either in line or in column of sections. Column of pieces is never used, but in passing a defile, or on a march, or moving into or out of a park.

A piece with four horses and its prolonge extended, occupies forty-four feet, and this interval must be preserved between the piece in line. A piece is in line when the horses' heads are towards the enemy and the leading horses of the caisson are forty-five paces from the muzzle (or rear) of the gun.

A piece is in battery when its muzzle is towards the enemy and the horses to the rear.

The term "unlimber" is to detach the gun from the front wheels and the horses, so that it may be manœuvred by the gunners.

To *limber* is to again attach it for moving.

A non-commissioned officer has charge of each piece and each caisson, and directs their movements.

The caisson contains the ammunition.

The exercise of casemate guns and guns *en barbette*, in our fortifications, consists in loading and firing. There is no manœuvring as in the field.

An embrasure is the opening in the walls of a fort, through which the guns project.

Loop-holes are small openings through which musketry is fired.

A casemate is the stone roof under which the guns stand; the roof, being arched and of great thickness, protects the gunners from shot and shell. The gun so protected is termed a casemate gun. Barbette guns are those which are placed on top of the fortress, without shelter overhead from an enemy's fire. The advantage of them over casemate guns is, that they have a greater sweep of fire from right to left.

A half-plunging fire of guns in battery on the field may be obtained by posting them on sods six feet square by two and a half deep, with stakes driven around the square, to keep the sods compact and in place. An inclined plane should be constructed in the rear. In an open level country this position would be of great advantage, and is but the work of a few moments to cut, lay, and stake the sod.

The range of an ordinary gun, not rifled, can be increased by simply greasing a few inches of the interior of the bore near the mouth with a piece of pork rind.

☞ The friction primer and the percussion primer are probably the best tubes for artillery. They seldom miss fire. The essential point is certainty of ignition.

☞ The ordinary twelve-pound howitzers weigh from 430 to 750 pounds each. Twenty-four pounders about 1,200 pounds.

☞ When a crisis arrives at any one point on the

field in time of action, the movements of artillery should be such as to concentrate at that point with all possible despatch.

☞ Shrapnell is of special form, and sometimes made oblong. Each case for a twelve-pounder contains about 80 (4⅔ pounds) balls. In twenty-four's the number is 175 (10¼ pounds) balls.

☞ In howitzers the velocity given to shrapnell is one thousand feet per second; therefore, at that distance, one second fuze is required.

☞ The effective range of ordinary field-pieces is 1,300 yards.

☞ Never destroy your aim by being too hasty in firing.

☞ The mortar was first used afloat in 1679 at the French attack on Algiers.

☞ Sixteen hundred feet per second is the maximum velocity which it is ever considered expedient to give a cannon ball.

☞ Balls of a low velocity are retarded by the action of the air less than those of high velocity. The velocity of a ball depends upon the quantity and strength of powder by which it is projected.

☞ Gunpowder is composed of nitre, carbon, and sulphur—or saltpetre, charcoal and sulphur; 75 parts, in weight, of saltpetre, 15 of charcoal, and 10 of sulphur make the best gunpowder.

☞ Shot are cast from soft iron of good quality. If cast from hard, brittle iron they are more likely to break than penetrate when fired against hard bodies.

☞ Moulds for casting shot are sometimes of sand, and sometimes of iron. The former is preferred, because it produces smoother and less defective shot.

☞ The windage of a shot is the difference between its diameter and the diameter of the bore of its gun.

☞ There are two kinds of wads in common use for artillery, the junk wad and the grommet wad. The former is of junk, and the latter of rope. A wad simply to put over a shot and keep it in place had perhaps better be soft.

Part Third.

HINTS ON SURGERY.—ANTIDOTES FOR POISON, &c.

FOR ARRESTING THE FLOW OF BLOOD.

THERE are two sorts of blood vessels in the human body, the one composed of arteries which carry the blood from the heart to every part of the body, and the other of the veins, which returns the same blood, after the oxygen has been exhausted from it. The blood in the arteries is a bright red color, and in the veins of a darker hue.

Fortunately, arteries forcibly torn or lacerated are not apt to throw out blood, owing, says an eminent medical writer, to the vessels being paralyzed to a certain extent by the shock, so that it does not contract to force along the current of blood, which consequently coagulates and fills up the orifice of the wounded artery. It should be remembered that the blood is flowing from the heart and if therefore you make compression between the wound and the heart, by tying a handkerchief tightly round the limb, you will effectually check the bleeding for the time until a surgeon's assistance can be obtained.

A knot should be made in the handkerchief and placed directly over the main artery of the limb, bringing the ends around and tying them. Suppose a wound in the foot, leg, thigh, or arm, which bleeds profusely, should accidentally occur to some one in your presence, if assistance is not rendered at once as above described a life may be lost, when a little care would have saved it. No wound ought to be stuffed with rags, or any irritating application be made.

Sometimes the orifice of the wounded vessel may be visible. Compression directly over it with the ball of the thumb, until a surgeon arrives, will arrest the flow of blood.

Should one not be obtained at the instant, put a ligature around it in the following manner: Take a large needle and, placing the end in which the eye is into a piece of wood or cork, so that it will serve as a handle, hold the sharp end into a fire, or lighted pine, until it can be bent into a hook, then wipe away the blood, so as to render the orifice of the bleeding artery perfectly visible, and pass the hook gently through it and draw it gently out, and with a piece of strong silk or linen thread tie it around the edge with such a knot as will not slip. The surgeon can easily remove it, if upon his arrival he should think advisable so to do.

If the orifice is small, lacerate the end with a knife or by twisting it, in which state the artery will not bleed.

Profuse bleeding from wounds in the scalp, or face, or flesh wounds in other parts of the body may be arrested by lint, or compresses made of folded cotton, or linen wet in cold water and bound, or held firmly over the wound.

Castile soap is suitable to wash wounds with, for it is healing and soothing in its tendencies. Avoid touching wounds with all irritating substances.

For fractures, bind up the parts and apply cold water freely till you receive surgical aid.

For gun-shot wounds, outside applications of lint are excellent till you receive assistance. Washing with castile soap is good for blistered face or feet.

POISONED WOUNDS.

Poisoned wounds should be speedily exposed, and if the wound be on either of the extremities a handkerchief or cord should be placed around the limb between the wound and the heart, drawn tightly and tied. The wound should be sucked by the person himself, or some one present, taking care that there be no sores or scratch in the mouth of the person by whom it is done.

As soon as possible, the wound should be cut out, but this should not be attempted by an unprofessional person. The wound should be touched in every part by caustic of some sort, or, what is better, seared over with a hot iron.

For a rattlesnake, moccasin, or copper-headed snake sting, drink whiskey to excess, or if you can procure the cedran-bean make a tea out of it, and drink a half-pint of it every half-hour. In six hours you will be entirely cured. Suck and sear the wound also, as above described.

INSECTS IN THE EAR OR NOSE.

These may be ejected by a stream of warm water, cold will answer at a pinch, thrown in by means of a small syringe, or squirted by a companion through a reed or any small tube. The insect should not be picked at, as it will cause irritation and swelling.

ANTIDOTES FOR POISON.

The first thing that is to be done where it is ascertained a poison has been swallowed, is to endeavor to eject the substance from the stomach. An emetic may be instantly made of warm water and mustard. Excessive drinking of strong coffee afterwards is a good antidote. Milk and the whites of eggs are also excellent antidotes.

Poisoned oak, or vines, touching the skin, create irritation and discharges. They may be cured by applications of sulphur, mixed to the consistency of a paste with milk, and spread over the surface fresh every day till healed. In the absence of sulphur, gunpowder and water are a pretty good substitute.

SIGNS OF REAL DEATH FROM SUSPENDED ANIMATION.

Apparent death is not unfrequent from accidental blows or falls, from drowning, vapor of charcoal, or from narcotic poison.

Fatal results have taken place from want of knowledge, no doubt.

One of the most certain signs of death, is stiffness of the corpse; but it happens sometimes that this sign manifests itself during life. When a member is stiff from tetanus, convulsions, &c., it is difficult to change its position; and when it is done, it soon returns to its former state. In the stiffness of death, this is not the case, the member remaining as last placed. Stiffness from fainting fits takes place at once—stiffness of a corpse not till some time after death, when there is no longer heat in the body. The more sudden the death, the slower rigidity takes place.

If an individual who is thought to be dead is cold and soft, while there should be a certain degree of stiffness, his interment ought not to be hastened. Before deciding, a muscle of the arm or thigh ought to be laid bare, and electrified by a galvanic battery. If it gives a sign of contraction, life is extinct.

The sign of death most certain is *well-marked putre-faction;* but it does not belong to the unprofessional to decide; the *physician alone can establish this fact.*

The state of the face has been regarded as a sign of real death, viz.: forehead wrinkled and dry, eyes sunk, nose pointed, temples shrunk, ears drawn back, lips hanging, cheeks sunk, &c. Taken by itself, this sign is of no value, for it has been observed in persons twenty-four or forty-eight hours before death, and often it is wanting in persons who have died suddenly.

Absence of the circulation, of feeling the beating of

the heart and pulsation of the arteries, have been regarded as infallible means of deciding if the individual is dead; but it is fully proved that a person may live many hours without its being possible to perceive the least movement in the parts spoken of.

An individual has been considered as dead *when he ceases to breathe.* Many expedients have been resorted to, but experience proves that none of these signs are sufficient to establish the reality of death.

It has been thought that the individual is dead when he is cold, and lives if he preserves warmth. This sign is of the least value, for drowned persons who can be restored are ordinarily cold, while those suffocated preserve heat even a long time after death.

Incisions, burns, blisters, &c., sometimes employed, ought to be considered secondary, as experience proves that in certain diseases the sensibility is so destroyed that the patients do not feel any pain, even for several days after these applications.

The conclusion is that no one of the signs enumerated is sufficient for pronouncing a person dead.

That death ought to be regarded as real in an individual who combines all these signs.

Part Fourth.

CAVALRY AND CAVALRY MOVEMENTS.

CAVALRY AND CAVALRY MOVE-MENTS.

IT can hardly be expected that the militia or volunteer cavalry are to be instructed in all the varied movements and details as practised by regular cavalry. The large sums of money required by volunteer mounted regiments to maintain themselves on any thing like an efficient footing, and in the care, equipments, and furnishing forage for their animals, deter many persons from joining such organizations. In time of peace, moreover, their services are seldom required, except it may be to quell a riot or suppress a violent mob, which can be accomplished as effectually by infantry with the bayonet. Probably more for these reasons than any others, we hear of but few formations of cavalry regiments, as compared with the number of infantry and rifles organized in the more densely populated States. The States adjoining the frontiers of the Indian country frequently muster into their service mounted rangers for the purpose of suppressing Indian depredations, and to follow up the savages into their fastness, in the absence of regularly equipped troops of the Government. These rangers, however, never find it necessary, in carrying on this system of warfare, to perfect themselves in all the minutiæ and movements as prescribed by army regulations. They are mounted more particularly for active pursuit, and armed with all sorts of weapons that may come to hand, and ride as best suits the convenience of each ranger, without regard to system or drill.

With the regular cavalry the case is far different. They are compelled to go through a thorough course of instruction. They must learn to mount and dismount with ease; to sit a horse naturally, and to have the stirrups sufficiently short to enable them to command their horses, and to rise in them to strike when it may be necessary to use the sword or lance.

The manœuvres are simple with the sword or lance, and can easily be learned. The exercise with the sword is reduced to a very few motions, as follows:

Draw—SWORDS.—At this command carry the right hand over the reins; run the hand to the wrist through the sword-knot; grasp the sword and draw it six inches out of the scabbard.

Draw the sword briskly, carry it to the right shoulder, point upwards; drop the hand on the upper part of the right thigh, the little finger on the outside of the gripe, and the back of the blade in the hollow of the shoulder. This is the position of *Carry*—SWORD.

Slope—SWORDS.—Loosen the grasp of the handle, advancing at the same time the sword hand, with the wrist turned up, so as to allow the back of the sword to rest on the shoulder in a sloping position.

Carry—SWORDS.—Draw the hand to its position so as to allow the sword to resume its perpendicularity.

Raise—SWORDS—*as front rank.*—Raise the sword hand (right hand) perpendicularly and bring it as high as the chin, blade to the left and fingers opposite the face, which is the position preparatory *to give point.* Raise the wrist to the height of the eyes—the arm half extended—the edge turned towards the right, and the point a little lower than the wrist.

As rear rank.—Raise the sword, the arm half extended, the wrist a little above the head, the edge upwards, the point backwards, and about one foot above the wrist. These are the positions of the sword by the two ranks just before the charge, and at the shock when the men are to give point, or cut and use their swords as they see fit, after breaking the line of an enemy.

Carry—SWORDS.—Bring the sword to its original position on the right thigh.

Return—SWORDS.—Raise the sword perpendicularly; the flat to the front, edge to the left, the thumb to the height of the chin and about six inches from it. Carry the wrist near and opposite to the left shoulder, drop the point, turn the head to the left, return the sword to its scabbard, bringing the head again to the front and the right hand to its position by the thigh.

Pistol and carbine should be used by every man as may be most convenient to him.

4

In cavalry, the same as in infantry, a rank is any number of men, side by side in a line.

Cavalry are said to be marching by *files*, when each front rank man has his rear rank man following him, the whole in one single string.

By *Twos.*—When each front rank *two* has its rear rank *two* following, it being a column of two abreast.

By *Fours.*—When each front rank *four* has its rear rank *four* by its side, being a column eight abreast.

Sections of fours.—When each front rank *four* has its rear rank *four* following, it being a column four abreast.

A Platoon is the fourth part of a squadron. Platoons in squadron are numbered 1st, 2d, 3d, 4th, from the right.

A Troop (horse company) is the half of a squadron, two troops making one squadron. Troops are right and left in each squadron.

A Squadron.—Two or more squadrons compose a corps, or brigade, numbered 1, 2, 3, &c., from the right.

A Division.—Two or more brigades compose a division.

Close order.—The ordinary distance at which the rear rank is formed behind the front rank is *one yard*, or pace.

Open order.—The increased distance taken by the rear rank on some occasions of parade—is *six yards*, or paces.

Front.—The distance towards which the line faces when formed—the extent from flank to flank—that is, the breadth. The extent of front of a squadron is to be calculated at about as many yards as it contains files.

Depth.—The distance from front to rear.

PLATOON — 1/4 squadron # 1st 2nd 3rd 4th
TROOP — 1/2 squadron
SQUADRON - 2+ = CORPS OR BRIGADE
DIVISION = 2+ Brigades

Distance.—The space between one brigade and another in column. From one horse to another, when marching in file, twos, fours, or sections of fours—the distance should be one yard. From one squadron to another in close column, ten yards. The depth of two ranks, taking the length of the fullest-sized cavalry horses at eight feet, and the distance between the ranks at three feet, is to be reckoned at about nineteen feet.

Intervals are spaces between squadrons and brigades in line; those between squadrons should not exceed ten paces, and those between brigades not over fifteen paces.

PACES.

There are three paces in cavalry tactics: the walk, the trot, and the gallop. The walk should be made at the rate of three and a half to four miles an hour, the trot at eight and a half an hour, and the gallop at eleven miles an hour. The gallop is not considered applicable to general purposes of manœuvre, though it may be used for very simple formations.

The rate of charge should not exceed the speed of the slowest horses, except in cases of great emergency when the fastest will push for the front rank and hurry forward with their comrades.

To preserve uniformity of movement, the trot and gallop should commence gradually and by the whole body at the same time.

The term pace, by which distance and intervals are measured, is one yard.

COMMANDS

are of two kinds, those of caution and those of execution. They should be given in a firm and clear voice, and repeated by the chiefs of subdivisions.

MOUNTING.

Stand to Horse.—The position of the man is on the left side of the horse, square to the front, toe on a line with the horse's fore foot; right hand back upwards, holding the rein of the snaffle over the curb, six inches from the ring of the bit, left hand hanging down by the side.

Prepare to Mount.—Face to the right, take the curb rein in the left hand, run down the left hand to the neck of the horse, still holding the bridle, and seize with the fore-fingers of the left hand a lock of the mane about a foot from the saddle; seize the stirrup strap with the right hand, place the left foot in the stirrup and shift the right hand to the cantle (back) of the saddle, taking a firm hold.

Mount.—At this command, spring with the right foot, and support the body with the left foot in the stirrup, throw the right leg over the horse's back, seat yourself in the saddle, and place the right foot in its stirrup without the aid of hand or eye.

POSITION ON HORSEBACK.

The body should be balanced in the middle of the saddle, head up and square to the front, left hand holding the reins, back of the hand uppermost, on a line with the elbow; the right hand hanging by the left thigh; legs hanging straight down from the knee, near the horse's sides, and the toes raised slightly from the insteps, and as near the horse's sides as the heels.

DISMOUNT.

Prepare to dismount, is the first command. *Dismount*, the second. Bring the right leg clear over the horse's back, and dismount, and *stand to horse.*

POSTS OF OFFICERS AND OTHERS IN COLUMN.

Columns of twos or fours.—Right in front.

The colonel abreast with the centre of the brigade, eight yards from the left flank of the column. The lieutenant-colonel and major on the same flank, the first abreast with the centre of the two first squadrons, and the last abreast with the centre of the two last squadrons. The adjutant on the same flank, abreast with the leading files. The sergeant-major in rear of the column, except when the left is in front, when he is on the right flank, abreast with the leading files. The chiefs of squadrons on the left flank, opposite to the centre of their commands; the juniors on the right flank. The chiefs of the leading companies of squadrons in front of their commands, and the chiefs of the other companies on the left of their leading files.

The file-closers on the right flank of the column, abreast with the files they cover when in line. The trumpets should be six yards in advance of the officers at the head of the column.

THE CHARGE, OR ATTACK OF CAVALRY.

The charge is regulated by the principles of the direct march, but is more animated and impetuous. It should commence with a brisk trot, then a gallop, constantly increasing in velocity as the men approach the enemy. To render it effective, the attack must be made with a rush and a bold, determined front. There are three modes of charging, viz.: in a line parallel or oblique to the front of the enemy, by echelon, and in column.

The charge should be sounded by all the trumpets. As the men near the enemy, they rise in their stirrups, lowering the bridle hand, (left hand,) but keep command of their horses, as well as the line of their rank, and thus throw themselves upon the enemy; the front rank with their swords pointed forward, immediately before the shock, and the rear rank with the sword *raised*. The enemy being routed, the commanding officer orders the trumpeters to sound the *rally*, when each man pulls up and joins his standard. As it is important that the enemy should not have time to rally, the flank platoons of each squadron, or some others, are sent in pursuit.

To recall them the *rally* is again sounded, when they return to their respective squadrons. The charge ought always to be anticipated, if possible, as there is imminent danger of being overthrown by receiving a charge at a halt. A skilful commander is always on the alert on the field of battle, to guard against surprise while at a halt. Were he taken so by a column of the enemy's cavalry, it would be almost impossible to resist it. Where cavalry are operating against each other, a charge should always be met by a charge. If a smaller number are about being attacked, a good plan is, to put their horses to an easy gallop, make a feint at receiving the charge of the enemy by a counter-charge, and when within say twenty or thirty yards of the front rank of the enemy deliver your fire from your small-arms, each shot converging towards the *centre* of the enemy's column. The next movement is to replace your fire-arms, instantly seize your swords, divide the command into three or four attacking parties, wheel to the right and left, so as to avoid the shock of the enemy in front, and attack him determinedly on each flank. The movement must be executed with great quickness. You are supposed to be at an easy gallop when you deliver your fire, while the enemy is rushing towards you with their horses on the full jump. The very instant you fire, hurry to the attack on his flanks, before he can stop the momentum of his speed and face about to repel you. Keep playing on his flanks in this manner, by retreating and repeating the movement, and if you do not succeed in defeating him, owing to his superior numbers, you may at least increase your own effectiveness one-third more than you could hope to do by receiving the shock in front. Of course such a movement as the one we allude to is based upon the supposition that the horses of the enemy, as well as your own, are nearly, if not quite equal in speed. You are supposed to have greater command over your own horses at any easy gallop than your enemy, who is charging directly on you at top speed. You could, therefore, wheel to the right or left quicker, and get to his flanks before he could pull up and change his direction to follow you. If his front rank pulled up too suddenly, they would be in danger of being overridden by their rear ranks, and plunged into hopeless confusion. If the speed and mettle of your animals are still greater than the enemy's, then the advantages are more in your favor for a successful issue.

Chiefs of squadrons charge at the head of their respective squadrons. The colonel at the head of such squadron as he may think his presence most necessary. The lieutenant-colonel and major at the head of other squadrons of their wing. Adjutants, sergeant-majors, and general guides keep their places as in line. The trumpets in the rear of the centre, with the trumpet-major at their head, unless the colonel shall see fit to have him near his person. All orders are given through the trumpeters.

When using pistol or carbine, the fire should be delivered as close as possible to the enemy's line, and without taking time to reload, the pistol should be replaced in its holster, the carbine swung round to the back, and

SHORT RIFLE OR MUSKET

the sword, which should be kept dangling by the right wrist, meanwhile be instantly seized, and used for either cut or thrust.

When a charge is unsuccessful at the first onset, the retreat may be sounded, that the squadrons may reform and fall back under cover of the artillery, in good order, or to prepare for a second or third attack, as the commander may desire. If they cannot succeed in penetrating the enemy's line, they should retire manœuvring.

BREECH-LOADING WEAPONS.

PREFERENCE

Breech-loading carbines, or rifles with the Maynard primer (tape cap), are handled and loaded with far more facility on horseback than the old-fashioned musketoons formerly used by cavalry, or pieces of any sort which are loaded at the bore.

The former can be loaded and fired at least four or five times to one of the latter. With the patent primer, too, the annoyance and oftentimes delay, while mounted and your horse in motion, of placing a cap on the nipple of your piece are avoided, and the danger of losing the cap obviated. There is no drawing of rammer, ramming home cartridge, and returning rammer, with breech-loading weapons, and the preference therefore should always be given them, when they can be obtained, for mounted service. The American Government has adopted them for its regular cavalry, as we believe also the leading governments of Europe for the same corps of their armies. The revolving rifle comes under the head of breech-loading. The only difference between it and the carbine is, that the revolving rifle has a chamber to it similar to the common revolver, and carries six, and some of them even more charges at once, which must be discharged successively before being replenished; whereas the carbine, or Sharp's rifle, can only contain one cartridge at a time. We would recommend the latter, with Maynard primer, for mounted corps, as they are less liable to get out of order. Another thing which should be taken into consideration is, that breech-loading small-arms are not so apt to burst as those loaded at the bore. The cartridge is always "home" the very instant it is placed in the piece, and the lever, which opens the small aperture at the breech to admit it, is closed. There are only two motions required in loading. At the first, *handle cartridge —load*, jerk back the lever, and insert the cartridge in the breech; and at the second command, *ready*, close the lever with the forefinger of the right hand, which, as it comes back to its position, cuts the end of the cartridge, and then with your thumb cock the piece—a cap appears over the nipple as you pull back the cock, and you are all ready for immediate firing.

TRAINED HORSES FOR CAVALRY.

To prevent your horse shying, or becoming unmanageable by bolting, or rearing, or pitching in the face of an enemy's fire, he should be thoroughly broken and trained. He should be taught all the simple movements of the troop, and to obey them if possible at the sound of the trumpet; also familiarize him by firing blank cartridges over his head, in front of his face and alongside of his ears, and to wheel to the right or left with you by a pressure of your knee on his sides. These can all be accomplished with very little trouble by any person of ordinary intelligence. Many a trooper's life has been saved on the field of battle by the sagacity of his horse, in obeying the calls of the trumpeters, and numerous instances are on record where riderless they have charged with the squadrons they belonged to into a mass of infantry, and by indulging in the most vigorous kicks and art of biting, placed many of the enemy *hors d'combat*. In some portions of Europe, cavalry horses are trained to wheel and kick with both hind feet, and follow it up by a succession of kicks directly at the front of an enemy's square.

They should also be trained to leap a piece of artillery while being fired, a hedge or a ditch, to make them entirely serviceable in time of action, and be ready for all emergencies that might arise; attention and proper care should also be paid to their grooming, and see that their forage is not musty and damp. They should never be picketed or " hobbled," if it can be avoided, on wet or marshy land, or to stand exposed to cold winds without being blanketed, or to the heat of the sun in warm weather, when a shady place under a tree is near at hand. After a long march, a little dung applied to the bottom of their hoofs, and permitted to remain there for a few hours, will have a tendency to draw off all inflammation about the frog and pastern joint, and greatly relieve your animal. It may be retained in its place by a piece of rag or canvas; and when these cannot be obtained it would be well to wash their legs in the nearest stream.

SABRE CUTS.

There are seven cuts with the sabre: one with the right hand, even with the left shoulder, edge of the blade to the front, and throw the arm by the right hip backwards; second, turn the hand and sweep the blade back again, cutting half downwards; third and fourth, the same movement on the left side of you, the sabre directed from above the right shoulder, turning the body half round to the left; the other cuts are made to the right and left, at direct right angle with your body.

The great St. George cut is performed by carrying the right hand to the left shoulder, and sweeping the sabre swiftly around to the right, extending the arm full length, half turning the body to the right at the instant, and describe a half-circle with the point of your sabre.

The force of a blow with the sabre is greater within eight inches of the point, than half-way to the guard.

SKIRMISHING.

The principal duty of a mounted skirmisher, is to gain time, while the main body to which he is attached, can prepare for action, and to watch the movements of the enemy, to keep him in check, and to prevent him from approaching so close to the main body, as to annoy them in any manner, until they are ready to receive his attack.

On service, regularity in skirmishing, and correctness of distance cannot always be maintained, on account of the movements of the enemy and the nature of the ground, and sometimes other unforeseen circumstances.   On ordinary occasions a few mounted men may be sufficient for this duty, yet it is not an unfrequent occurrence to call into requisition entire squadrons to act as skirmishers.

They should always move out and return at a gallop, and keep their horses in motion, to avoid becoming a mark to the enemy.

Part Fifth.

ORDER OF ENCAMPMENT FOR ARTILLERY, CAVALRY, AND INFANTRY, AND GENERAL DETAILS OF CAMP DUTY, COOKING, &c.

ORDER OF ENCAMPMENT.

FOR INFANTRY.

The troops are on all occasions to be encamped in the order of battle.

The front of the camp of a regiment of 1,000 men in two ranks will be 400 feet.

The companies will encamp in the street perpendicularly to the line in which they were drawn up—facing to the color line.

Each street in a large encampment should have some designated number or name posted up, on a flag, or some conspicuous place, to the right and left of the line, that it may be more readily known.

The width of the *main* street should not be over *forty* feet, or less than *fifteen*.

The interval between the ranks of tents is *two* paces; between the files of tents of adjacent companies, *two* paces.

Between regiments, *twenty-two* paces.

The color line is *ten* paces in front of the front rank of tents.

in charge of CLOTHING, rations providing quarters, and other supplies

The kitchens are *twenty* paces behind the rear rank of company's tents.

SELLING ITEMS

The non-commissioned staff and sutler, *twenty* paces in the rear of the kitchens.

The company officers, *twenty* paces further in rear.

The field and staff officers, *twenty* paces in rear of the company officers.

The company officers are in rear of their respective companies.

The colonel and lieutenant-colonel are near the centre of the line of field and staff.

The adjutant, a major, and surgeon on the right.

The quartermaster, a major, and assistant-surgeon on the left.

The advanced post of the police guard is about *two hundred* paces in front of the color line, and opposite the centre of the regiment, or on the best ground.

The prisoners' tent *four* paces in rear of police guard.

In a regiment of the second line, the advanced post of the police guard is *two hundred* paces in rear of the line of its field and staff.

The horses of the staff officers, and of the baggage train, are *twenty-five* paces in rear of the tents of the field and staff.

The wagons are parked on the same line, and the men of the train camped near them.

The sinks of the men are *one hundred* and *fifty* paces in front of the color line.

Those of the officers, *one hundred* paces in rear of the train.

The sinks should always be hid from public view, by encircling them with bushes, or other blinds, a portion of the earth dug out of them ought every day to be thrown in to cover the filth.

When convenient, the sinks of the men may be placed in rear, or on a flank.

CAMP OF CAVALRY.

In the cavalry service, each company has one file of tents—the tents opening on the street facing the left of the camp.

The horses of each company are placed in a single file, facing the opening of the tents, and are fastened to pickets planted firmly in the ground, from *three* to *six* paces from the tents of the troops.

The interval between the file of tents should be such that, the regiment being broken into column of companies, each company should be on the extension of the line on which the horses are to be picketed.

The streets separating the squadrons are wider than those between the companies, by the interval separating squadrons in line ; these intervals are kept free from any obstruction throughout the camp.

The horses of the rear rank are placed on the left of those of their file-leaders.

The horses of the lieutenants are placed on the right of their platoons.

Those of the captains, on the right of the company.

Each horse occupies a space of *two* paces.

The number of horses in the company fixes the depth of the camp, and the distance between files of tents.

The forage is placed between the tents.

The kitchens are *twenty* paces in front of each file of tents.

The non-commissioned officers are in the tents of the front rank.

Camp followers, teamsters, &c., are in the rear rank.

The police guard in the rear rank, near the centre of the regiment.

The tents of the lieutenants are *thirty* paces in rear of the file of their company.

The tents of the captains, *thirty* paces in rear of the lieutenants.

The colonel's tent *thirty* paces in rear of the captains, near the centre of the regiment.

The lieutenant-colonel on his right, the adjutant on his left; the major's on the same line, opposite the second company on the right and left; the surgeon on the left of the adjutant.

The field and staff officers have their horses on the left of their tents, on the same line with the company horses.

Sick horses are placed in one line, on the right or left of the camp. The men who attend them have a separate file of tents; the forages and wagons in rear of this file. The horses of the train and of camp followers are in one or more files, extending to the rear, behind the right or left squadron. The advance police guard is *two hundred* paces in front, opposite centre of regiment, the horses in one or two files.

Sinks for the men 150 paces in front. Officers, 100 paces in rear of the camp.

CAMP OF ARTILLERY.

Artillery is encamped near the troops to which it is attached, so as to be protected from attack, and to contribute to the defence of the camp.

Sentinels for the park are furnished by the artillery, and when necessary by the other troops.

For a battery of six pieces the tents are in three files, one for each section; distance between the ranks of tents, 15 paces, tents opening to the front.

The horses of each section (two guns) are picketed in one file, 10 paces to the left of the file of tents.

In the horse-artillery, or if the number of horses makes it necessary, the horses are in two files, on the right and left of the file of tents.

The tents of the officers are in the outside files of company tents, 25 paces in rear of the rear rank—the captain on the right, the lieutenants on the left.

The *park* is opposite the centre of the camp, 40 paces in rear of the officers' tents. The carriages in files, 4 paces apart; distance between ranks of carriages sufficient for the horses when harnessed to them. The park guard is 25 paces in rear of the park.

Sinks for the men 150 paces in front.

Officers, 100 paces in rear.

The harness is kept in the tents of the men, ready for immediate use.

BIVOUACS.

A bivouac means sleeping on the earth without tents. A fire for each platoon is made, and the men lie around it, with their arms ready, to repel a night assault of the enemy.

In stormy weather, a shelter should be made, if possible, with stakes, driven in the ground, and a slight structure overhead, the whole covered in with bushes and branches of small trees.

CANTONMENTS.

In cantonments, the cavalry should be placed under shelter, whenever the distance from the enemy, and from the ground where the troops are to form for battle, permits it.

-A place for assembling is selected by the colonel in case of alarm.

Farm-yards, sheds, and barns, when in close proximity to a cantonment, may be used for shelter.

When cavalry and infantry canton together, the latter furnish guards by night, and the former by day.

Troops cantoned in presence of an enemy should be covered by advanced guards, and natural or artificial obstacles, such as a river-ditch, with a few pieces of artillery posted covering the approaches or ford.

DRILL AND EXERCISES IN CAMP.

When troops remain in camp or cantonments for several days, they should be exercised daily in drill and manœuvring, for two or three hours.

ORDERS.

When in the field, verbal orders and sealed orders are carried by officers. When orders are carried by orderly sergeants, the place and time of departure should be marked on them, and place and hour of delivery on the receipt which is returned to the officer sending the order.

WATCHWORDS.

The countersign and parole are issued daily from head-quarters, and, if necessity requires, two and three times a day. The countersign is given to the sentinels and non-commissioned officers of the guard. The parole to the commissioned officers of guards. The parole is usually named after a general. The countersign, of a regiment or battle, or some simple word.

Both the parole and countersign should be given to none but officers, non-commissioned officers, and sentinels of the guard.

If an officer or private has leave to go beyond the line of pickets, or to an outpost, or is sent to carry some order beyond the lines, he is usually intrusted with the countersign, to enable him to pass the guard.

Thus, if he was returning, and was hailed by the picket (or guard) with the words *halt—who goes there?* he would instantly respond *officer*, (or messenger, or friend, whatever he may be.)

Sentinel.—Advance, officer, with the countersign.

--The officer advances within four paces; the sentinel, meanwhile, cocking his piece, brings it to a *ready*, to guard against surprise. Sentinel lowers his piece to a charge bayonet, and bids officer to *stand.* The officer then utters the countersign in a low voice. If it is correct, the sentinel then half-cocks his piece, and brings it to a shoulder, and says *pass*, when the officer passes inside the line. He is liable to be hailed two or three times, however, before he reaches his quarters, in which case the same ceremony is gone through with each and every time.

If the officer advances, and says he has no countersign, the sentinel immediately calls the guard, when the guard approach and take the officer into custody. Probably he may be a spy, or a deserter from the enemy. His true character, however, must be discovered before he is released.

If he attempts to run off after he is several times hailed with *who goes there?* or fails to answer, the sentinel is justified in shooting him, at the same time calling for the guard.

In no event should the sentinel quit his post while on duty, unless driven in by the enemy, when he will fire his piece at them, and retire to alarm the camp, post, or garrison.

If one of the guard desert, or it is believed the enemy knows the countersign, the officer of the guard on the spot will substitute another, and the fact must be immediately reported at head-quarters.

DETAILS FOR SERVICE.

Duties performed by detail are of four classes:

1st. Grand guards and outposts. 2d. Interior guards, as of magazines, hospitals, &c. 3d. Orderlies. 4th. Police guards.

POLICE GUARD.

A police guard is detailed every day from each regiment, consisting of two sergeants, three corporals, two drummers, and men enough to furnish the required sentinels and patrols. The men are taken from all the companies, according to their strength. The guard is commanded by a lieutenant. It furnishes ten sentinels at the camp, one over the arms of the guard, three on the color front, three fifty paces in rear of field-officers' tents, and one on each flank, between it and the next regiment. If it is a flank-regiment, one more sentinel is posted on the outer flank.

ADVANCED POST.

An advanced post is detached from the police guard. It consists of a sergeant, corporal, drummer, and nine men as sentinels and guard over the prisoners. Under no pretext must they leave the post. Their meals are sent to them.

OFFICER OF THE DAY.

The officer of the day is charged with the order, discipline and cleanliness of the camp. He orders the *calls* beaten by the drummer of the guard.

COLOR SENTINEL.

The sentinel over the colors will permit no one to remove them, except in presence of an escort; to let no one touch them, but the color-bearer, or the sergeant of the police guard, when he is accompanied by two armed men.

SUSPICIOUS PERSONS.

The sentinels on the front, flanks, and rear will permit no soldier to leave camp with horse or arms, unless conducted by a non-commissioned officer. Suspicious persons, prowling about the camp, will be arrested by them, and at night every one who attempts to enter, even the soldiers of other corps, if they have not a pass.

COLOR FRONT.

Sentinels on the color front will permit no arms to be removed from the stacks, without orders. The sentinel at the colonel's tent will notify him, if any unusual movement takes place about the camp.

PASSING OUT OF CAMP.

If any one is to be passed out of camp at night, the officer of the guard sends him under escort to the advanced post and the sergeant of the post has him passed over the chain of sentinels.

AT RETREAT.

At retreat, the officer of the guard has the roll of his guard called, and inspects arms, that they are in order and loaded, and visits the advanced posts for the same purpose. The colors are hauled down by the sergeant of the police guard, folded and laid on the trestle in rear of the arms. The sutlers' stores are closed, and the kitchen fires put out.

ROUNDS AND PATROLS.

Rounds and patrols are made at various times of the night by the officer and non-commissioned officers of the guard, to satisfy themselves of the vigilance of the police guard and sentinels.

AT REVEILLE. SIGNAL TO GET UP IN AM

Reveille is usually beaten at daybreak, when the police guard takes arms, the officer of the guard inspects it and the advanced post, and the sergeant replants the colors in place.

DOUBLE CHAIN OF SENTINELS.

When necessary, small outposts are stationed about the camp, forming what is called a double chain of sentinels. These posts are under the orders of the commander of the police force.

CAMPING PARTY.

When the camping party precedes the regiment, and the new police guard marches with the camping party, the guard, on reaching the camp, forms in line, thirty paces in front of the centre of the ground marked for the regiment. The officer of the guard furnishes the sentinels required.

PICKET OF A REGIMENT.

The picket of a regiment is a lieutenant, two sergeants, four corporals, a drummer, and about forty privates.

GRAND GUARDS.

Grand guards are the advanced posts of a camp, or cantonment, and are composed of cavalry and infantry, the cavalry furnishing the advanced sentinels. It is usually commanded by a captain. If there is no pass to be observed or defended, the guard is placed near the centre of the ground they are to observe.

In broken or mountainous countries where the inhabitants are hostile, intermediate posts should be established, if the grand guard is distant from the camp, to keep up communication with the main body. Grand guards watch the enemy in front. The camp must furnish additional guards to protect their rear and secure their retreat, when attacked.

VIDETTES.

Videttes are mounted patrols. Their duty is to watch the enemy, and should endeavor in turn not to be seen. Videttes carry their pistols or carbines in their hands.

A FLYING SENTINEL.

A flying sentinel is one who moves about on dark or stormy nights, examining the paths and hollows for an enemy.

CAVALRY PATROLS.

The duty of cavalry patrols is to examine a hostile country to a greater distance than infantry, and make known to the infantry guard all they observe. When patrols are sent beyond the advanced posts, the posts and sentinels should be informed.

CAMP FIRES.

There should be only one camp fire to each platoon. The fires of grand guards should be hid from view. At outposts liable to surprise, fires should not be permitted.

BEARERS OF FLAGS.

Bearers of flags are not permitted to pass the outer chain of sentinels. Their faces should be turned from the post, or army, and if necessary their eyes bandaged, that they may not witness the number and force of their adversaries.

APPOINTMENT OF ADJUTANTS.

Commanders of regiments appoint their own adjutants and non-commissioned staff of the regiment.

MARKED AND NUMBERED.

Every article except arms and accoutrements belonging to a regiment, should be marked with the name and number of the regiment.

Such articles belonging to companies, are to be marked with the letter of the company, in addition to the name and number of the regiment.

INSPECTION OF KITCHEN.

In camps or barracks company officers should inspect the kitchen daily, as to economy in cooking and cleanliness of the utensils.

MESS FURNITURE.

The only mess furniture of the soldier, is one tin plate, tin cup, knife, fork and spoon, to be carried by himself on the march.

COMPANY BOOKS.

The books allowed to each company are : one descriptive book, one clothing book, one order book, and one morning report book.

LAUNDRESSES.

Four women are allowed to each company as washerwomen, and receive one ration per day each.

ARRESTS.

None but commanding officers have power to place officers under arrest.

All prisoners without written charges preferred against them, will be released by the officer of the day at guard-mounting, unless the commanding officer orders their detention.

MILITARY HONORS AND SALUTES.

In saluting a general officer, it should be done by cavalry with sabres presented, trumpets sounding the march, all the officers saluting and standards dropping. By infantry with drums beating march, arms presented, colors dropping.

The President of the United States is to be saluted with the highest honors.

Guards turn out and present arms to general officers as often as they pass them.

To commanders of regiments, garrison or camp, their own guard turn out, and present arms once a day, after which they turn out with shouldered arms.

Officers when they pass each other should salute by touching the hat; inferiors always salute superiors first, which the latter should promptly return.

FUNERAL HONORS.

The funeral escort of a Commander-in-Chief consists of a regiment of infantry, squadron of cavalry, and battery of six pieces of artillery.

Major-General.—A regiment of infantry, squadron of cavalry, and four pieces of artillery.

Brigadier-General.—A regiment of infantry, troop of cavalry, and two pieces of artillery.

For a Colonel.—A regiment.

Lieutenant-Colonel.—Six companies.

Major.—Four companies.

Captain.—One company.

Subaltern.—Half a company.

The escort should always be commanded by an officer of the same rank with the deceased. If none be present, then the next inferior rank.

That of a Sergeant.—Of fourteen rank and file, commanded by a Sergeant.

Corporal.—Of twelve rank and file.

Private.—Of eight rank and file, commanded by a Corporal. For officers three volleys are fired over their graves.

PRISONERS OF WAR.

A report of prisoners, and of the number and description of the killed and wounded of the enemy, should be forwarded to the adjutant-general's office, Washington.

ARRANGEMENT OF TROOPS.

Arrangement of troops on parade and in order of battle, is: 1st, light infantry; 2d, infantry of the line; 3d, light cavalry; 4th, cavalry of the line; 5th, heavy cavalry; artillery and engineers are in the centre of the brigades or corps to which they are attached. Volunteers and militia take position on the left of the regular troops of the same arm.

MARCHES.

Cavalry and infantry do not march together, unless the proximity of the enemy makes it necessary. Batteries of artillery and their caissons move with the corps to which they are attached. The field train and ambulances march in rear of the column, and the baggage with the rear guard. When necessary, the orders specify the rations the men are to carry in their haversacks. The execution of marching orders should not be delayed. If the commander is not at the head of his troops when they are to march, the next in rank puts the column in motion. On the march no one shall fire a gun or cry *halt* or *march* without orders. Soldiers are not to stop for water, the canteens should be filled before starting. Halts to rest and re-form the troops are frequent during the day, depending on the object and length of the march. No honors are paid by troops on the march, or at halts. The sick march with the wagons.

ORDER OF BATTLES.

At proper distances from the enemy, the troops are formed for the attack in several lines. If only two can be formed, some battalions in column are placed behind the wing of the second line. The lines may be formed of troops in column or in order of battle, according to the ground and plan of attack. The reserve is formed of the best troops of foot and horse, to complete a victory, or make good a retreat. It is placed in the rear of the centre, or chief point of attack or defence. The cavalry should be distributed on the wings and at the centre, on favorable ground. In the attack, the artillery is employed to silence the enemy's batteries in position. In the defence, it is to direct its fire on advancing troops. In either case the fire of artillery should be concentrated. In battles and military operations, it is better to assume the offensive, and put the enemy on the defensive if possible; but to be safe in doing so requires a larger force than the enemy, or more favorable ground. If the attack of an enemy is repulsed, offensive operations against him must at once be taken. Soldiers must not leave the ranks to strip, or rob the dead, unless permission is given. The ambulance depot is generally established at some building nearest the scene of battle. A *red flag* is flying over it, to guide the ambulance wagons, and the wounded who can walk to it. After an action the munitions of war left on the field, are collected by the ordnance officers. Prisoners of war are disarmed and sent to the rear. The provost-marshal takes charge of prisoners.

QUARTERMASTER'S DEPARTMENT.

This department provides the quarters and transportation of the army, storage and transportation for all army supplies, clothing, camp and garrison equipage, cavalry and artillery horses, fuel, forage, straw, and stationery. He should take triplicate receipts for all his expenditures, and account for all disbursements made by him, &c., to head-quarters. He pays, also, all the incidental expenses of the army, of the pursuit and detection of deserters, burials of officers and soldiers, of spies and guides, medicines, &c., &c.

SUBSISTENCE DEPARTMENT.

The commissary attends to the subsistence of troops. The rations in the regular army are as follows: Three-

quarters of a pound of pork or bacon, or one and a
quarter pounds of fresh or salt beef; eighteen ounces of
bread or flour, or twelve ounces of hard bread, or one
and a quarter pounds corn meal; and at the rate, to one
hundred rations, of eight quarts of peas or beans, or in
lieu thereof, ten pounds of rice; six pounds coffee;
twelve pounds sugar; four quarts of vinegar; one and a
half pounds of tallow; one pound of sperm candles;
four pounds of soap; and two quarts of salt. Sometimes molasses, pickled onions, sour krout, fresh vege-
tables, dried apples or peaches, are substituted for some
of the regular rations.

MEDICAL DEPARTMENT.

This department is devoted exclusively to the sick and
wounded of the army.

PAY DEPARTMENT.

This department attends to the pay and accounts of
the officers and men.

DESERTERS.

Deserters are disarmed at the advanced posts, and
sent to the commanding officer of the guard, who ques-
tions them concerning the weakness of the enemy, the
position or strength of his forces. If many come in at
one time, they should be received cautiously, and only a
few together, the guard standing to arms meanwhile,

within a few paces. They are sent in the morning to the officer of the day, who conducts them before the colonel, or if attached to a brigade, to the brigade-general.

TO SALUTE WITH THE SWORD OR SABRE.

At the distance of six paces from the person to be saluted, raise the sword or sabre perpendicularly with the right hand, the point up, the flat of the blade opposite to the right eye, the guard at the height of the shoulder, and the elbow supported on the body. Drop the point of the sword or sabre in extending the arm, so that the right hand may be brought to the right thigh, and remain in that position until the person to whom the salute is rendered shall be passed, or shall have passed six paces.

COLOR SALUTES.

In the ranks the color-bearer salutes by gliding the right hand along the lance to the height of the eye, the heel of the lance remaining at the hip. Lower the lance by extending the right arm.

INSPECTION OF TROOPS.

The inspections of troops are generally preceded by a review. The inspecting officer requires every man to present a cleanly and soldierly appearance.

6

285274

SURGEON'S CALL.

When the surgeon's call is sounded, the sick able to go out, are conducted by the first sergeants of companies to the hospital.

DISCIPLINE.

To obtain the necessary amount of skill in firing a gun, or working a battery, a vast deal of exercising is necessary, alike for the officers to direct, and the men to execute the movements. A man must rely entirely for his safety upon the skill and promptitude of his movements for a successful issue. The multifarious and varied contingencies of actual service require that strict discipline should be had at all times.

A FLYING COLUMN.

A flying column is composed of light cavalry, light artillery, and light infantry or rifles, or either of them. They effect strategic movements, lay in ambuscades, cut off supplies, and take prisoners after a rout.

IN FIRING.

Great practice and judgment alone are required to do so accurately. The inclination of the ground should always be taken into consideration.

PRECEDENCE OF REGIMENTS AND CORPS.

The precedence of regiments and corps is as follows: 1st, light artillery; 2d, light dragoons; 3d, other regular cavalry; 4th, artillery; 5th, infantry; 6th, marine corps; 7th, riflemen; 8th, volunteer corps; 9th, the militia.

This order of precedence refers to parades. On all other occasions, the several regiments and corps are distributed as the commanding officer may judge best adapted to the service they are on.

DAILY DETAILS AND DUTIES.

The daily duty is announced in orders. In large camps there is a general officer of the day for each division; a field officer of the day for each brigade; a captain of the day for each regiment; and such general and regimental staff officers of the day as may be necessary to attend to the various details, and to receive and execute orders, according to their respective stations. In every regiment and garrison, besides the officer of the day, there should be detached daily, if the strength of the garrison will permit, a subaltern, four non-commissioned officers, a drummer, and such fatigue parties as circumstances may require.

The general of the day superintends the regularity and discipline of the camp. The field officer of the day superintends the camp of the brigade. The captain of the day, the cleanliness and regularity of the camp, or quarters of the regiment.

GUARDS.

The principal guards are:—1. Outposts and picket-guards.   2. Camp and garrison guards.   3. General officer's guard.

TRIMMINGS AND COLORS.

The color of the trimmings to the uniforms, as adopted for the various corps of the army, is as follows:

For artillerymen—scarlet.

Infantry—light, or sky-blue.

Riflemen—emerald-green, or medium.

Dragoons—orange.

Aides-de-camp—buff.

By observing the color of the soldiers' trimmings, one may easily distinguish to what branch of the service they belong.

DISTINGUISHING COLORS.

The garrison flag is the American flag.

For artillery—the regimental color is yellow.

For infantry—blue.

Cavalry—small guidons, half red and half white—the red uppermost.   The flag is swallow-tailed.

Flag of truce—white.

Surgeons' quarters—usually white.

CAMP SIGNALS.

The Reveille—is the signal to rise.
Peas upon a Trencher—call for breakfast.
The Troop—call for guard, and guard-mounting.
Roast Beef—the signal for dinner.
The Assembly—to form companies.
The Retreat—call for duty, and reading orders.
The Tattoo—the signal for retiring, and lights put out.
After which, none are allowed to leave the camp unless by special permission of the officer of the guard.

OFFICERS' BAGGAGE.

When troops are moving, officers' baggage is not allowed to exceed (mess-chest and all personal effects included) as follows :

General officers', 125 pounds.

Field officers', 100 pounds.

Captains', and other officers of the same and under rank, 80 pounds.

PRECAUTIONS.

If arms are taken apart to clean, it must be done by detachments successively, to guard against surprise.

☞ The number killed in war is small, compared to the large numbers carried off by disease, exposure, and other casualties incident to war, which may be guarded against by very simple precautions.

☞ Soups in the morning are preferable to coffee, and for this purpose the meat should be kept slowly stewing over night.

☞ When an army is not moving, rations are issued for four days at a time, commencing with companies to the right of a regiment, and finishing with the left company.

☞ Sentinels will fire on all persons, deserting to the enemy.

☞ In detached corps, small posts of picked men are at night sent forward to watch the enemy and give signal of his approach.

☞ Sentinels should be relieved every two hours, to keep them on the alert while on duty.

☞ With raw troops, or when the night is stormy and dark, sentinels should be doubled.

☞ A sentinel must be sure of the presence of an enemy, before he fires; once satisfied of that, he must fire, though all defence on his part is useless. The safety of the post depends upon his vigilance.

☞ General officers appoint their own *aides-de-camp*.

☞ Every soldier should have a company number.

☞ Deserters in time of war, if caught, are punished with death.

☞ One sutler is allowed for every regiment.

☞ Escorts of honor should be composed of cavalry or infantry, or both.

☞ In case of disorder, a sentinel must call out the guard.

☞ Inexperienced officers are put on guard as supernumeraries, for the purpose of instruction.

☞ General orders of commanders are numbered.

☞ In signing an official communication, the writer should annex to his name his rank and corps.

☞ Official letters should refer to one matter only.

☞ All communications on official service, should be marked on the cover " official business.".

☞ The formation by divisions is the basis of the organization and administration of armies in the field.

☞ Mixed brigades are often formed of infantry and light cavalry. They are used for advanced guards.

☞ Heavy cavalry belongs to the reserve.

☞ In military operations, brigades and divisions are designated by the officers commanding them.

☞ The grand depots of an army are established where the military operations would not expose them to be broken up.

☞ Reconnoissances should precede the establishment of the camp.

☞ The camping party of a regiment consists of the regimental quartermaster and quartermaster-sergeant, a corporal and two men per company.

☞ Fatigue parties are usually sent for supplies.

☞ The tents are arranged in ranks and files.

☞ The messes of prisoners should be sent to them by the cooks.

☞ *File left !* is the command to wheel to the left, and *file right !* the command to the right.

☞ Sergeants, like the rank and file, will always under arms, appear with bayonets fixed.

☞ Pioneers and drummers may be designated as markers, and used accordingly in the manœuvres and evolutions.

☞ Before forming a company, drill the men in squads.

☞ You can see a shell come towards you, but not a cannon ball; but when you fire a cannon ball, you can see it go from you.

TO PREPARE YEAST.

One handful hops, boiled half an hour in 2 quarts water.

10 potatoes, boiled half an hour and mashed; strain the water from the hops on the potatoes, stir in two tablespoonfuls of salt and 1 pint flour, set it to cool, add 1 pint brewers' yeast and let it rise 6 hours; strain and put into a tight stone jug.

TO MAKE BREAD.

3 quarts flour.

One half cup yeast.

1 tablespoonful of salt, and warm water, enough to make dough; knead, till smooth; get the flour off the sides of the pan, set in a warm place to rise over night; in the forenoon knead the dough, divide it, put it into pans, leave it to rise an hour, and bake it three-quarters of an hour.

MIXED BREAD.

1 Part rye meal.
1 Part Indian meal, scalded.
1 Part wheat flour.
Half-cup yeast, mix and set to rise eight hours, bake hot 40 minutes.

BISCUIT.

2 Quarts flour.
2 Ounces butter.
Half-pint boiling water.
1 Teaspoon salt.
1 Pint cold milk.
Half-cup yeast.
Mix well and set to rise, then mix a teaspoonful of saleratus in a little water, and mix into the dough, roll on a board an inch thick, cut into small biscuits and bake 20 minutes.

SLAPJACKS.

Take flour, little sugar and water, mix with or without little yeast, the latter better if at hand, mix into paste, and fry the same as fritters in clean fat, or butter.

SOUR MILK BISCUIT.

1 quart flour, 1 pint sour milk, 1 teaspoonful saleratus. Mix in the milk till it froths, stir it into the flour cold, mix quick and bake in the oven.

A SIMPLE SOUP.

Skim fat from mutton or beef steak, put it into a pot with 2 or 3 carrots, turnips, and onions, a cup of rice, the bones and bits of cold meat, pepper and salt, boil four hours, and then take out the bones.

COLD BEEF, BONES, BITS OF MEAT, &c.

Put them into a pot with 4 quarts of water, 2 or 3 carrots, turnips, onions, a few cloves, pepper and salt, boil four hours, strain and put back into the pot, mix a tablespoonful of flour with water. Stir it in and boil ten minutes.

USEFUL HINTS.

Drippings of beef and pork are nice to fry in, clarified. To clarify, put the drippings into an iron pot; to a quart of fat allow half a pint of cold water; let it boil till the water is boiled out, which may be known by its not bubbling. Strain it, and it is ready for use.

ROAST BEEF.

Roast ten minutes to every pound; don't salt or flour it till nearly done.

BEEF GRAVY.

Take drippings from the meat, put into a pan, and add a cup of boiling water; shake in a little flour and salt. Let it come to a boil, stirring it always.

A LEG OF MUTTON

should be roasted ten minutes to the pound. A shoulder the same, except half an hour less time to boil.

A BREAST OF VEAL

takes one and a half hours to roast. Lay a few strips of pork across. Stuff with bread, onions, and potatoes, chopped fine and seasoned.

TO BOIL RICE.

Wash clean two cupfuls, put it into a pot with two quarts of water, and boil it quite tender; drain, but do not stir it. Let it dry before the fire ten minutes. Every kernel will be separate, dry, and look white.

TO MAKE COFFEE.

Dry it in the oven, with the door open, one or two hours before roasting. When ready, set it on the fire, and stir till a light brown. One cup of ground will make one quart. Ten minutes are long enough to make good coffee.

TO MAKE TEA.

Put in the tea while the pot is hot; turn in just water enough to *wet* the tea, and let it stand five minutes, then fill it up with boiling water.

BREAD PUDDING.

Take a pound of stale bread; boil a quart of milk, pour it on and let it soak two hours; then rub it fine with the hands. Beat up five eggs and add them; and also a tablespoon of any kind of spice, two cups of sugar, and a little butter. Bake or boil two hours.

RICE PUDDING.

Mix three large spoonfuls of rice in a little cold milk; stir it into a quart of boiling milk; let it boil fifteen minutes. When cold, add a little lemon, sugar, and bake one hour.

Part Sixth.

ELEMENTARY PRINCIPLES OF THE MANUAL.—FORMATION OF COMPANY AND REGIMENT.

7

ELEMENTARY PRINCIPLES OF THE MANUAL.

POSITION OF THE RECRUIT.

AT the command ATTENTION! stand perfectly square, head erect, eyes direct to the front, arms allowed to fall naturally by the side, the thumb and two fingers turned slightly outwards; heels together, and toes four inches apart; knees straight, and body inclining a little forward.

The recruit should learn to assume this position with ease, and without stiffness.

Forward—MARCH!

At the command MARCH! he should invariably step with the left foot first, twenty-eight inches each step, considered a pace, without swaying the body or swinging the arms.

HALT!

At the command HALT! immediately draw up the right foot to the left, and come to a halt with the body erect, as in first position.

*Eyes—*RIGHT!

At the word RIGHT! turn the head gently to the right, and fix your eyes on a line with the eyes of those next to you in the same rank.

Front! Assume your former position, with eyes direct to the front.

*Eyes—*LEFT! The same movement, to the left.

Care should be taken not to swerve or move the body at any of these commands.

REST!

Draw the right foot a few inches to the rear of the left, leaning the weight of the body on the right foot, and cross the palm of the left hand over the back of the right hand, in front.

FACINGS!

Facing to the right is executed by placing the hollow of the right foot within an inch of the heel of the left foot. At the command *Right—*FACE! the recruit will wheel to the right, and then assume an erect position, drawing the heels close together.

*Left—*FACE! A reverse movement, to the left.

*About—*FACE!

At the word *About!* the left toe should be placed within an inch of the right heel; and at the second command, FACE! turn the body to the left on the heels, and face to the rear, bringing the heels again close together.

COMMON TIME.

Common time in marching is at the rate of ninety steps per minute.

DIRECT STEP.

The direct step is twenty-eight inches.

DOUBLE QUICK STEP.

The double quick step is thirty-three inches, and is made at the rate of one hundred and sixty-five steps per minute.

*Double quick step—*MARCH!

At the first command, the recruit will raise his hands closed, the fingers towards the body, to a level with the hips; the elbows to the rear, working free. At the second command, raise the left leg, the toe depressed, keeping step with those in the rank, and continue the movement till the command

HALT!

Immediately stop, drop the hands by the side, draw the heels together, and assume first position.

RUNNING.

The principles are the same as in double-quick step. Care should be taken to preserve the rank unbroken. Room should be afforded for free use of the limbs, without those in the rear, or to the right or left, pushing or crowding.

The breath may be recovered when the recruit is out of wind, by elevating the arms behind the head occasionally.   Relief may also be had by throwing the head upwards at times.

A SQUAD.

A squad consists of three or twelve men.

A RANK

is a straight line of a platoon, company, or battalion.

A FILE.

A line of men, one posted behind another.

A PLATOON.

Half a company.

A SECTION

Is half of a platoon.

A COMPANY

consists of seventy-four men, according to army regulation.   Company officers and sergeants are nine in number.

A REGIMENT.

Ten companies compose a regiment, or seven hundred and forty men.   Each company is named in alphabetical order—viz.: Co. A, B, C, D, E, F, G, H, J, K.   The whole commanded by a colonel.

A BATTALION

is half of a regiment, or two or five companies.

A BRIGADE.

Two regiments or more compose a brigade, commanded by a brigadier-general.

A DIVISION.

Two brigades to a division, commanded by a major-general.

A CORPS D'ARMÉE.

One or more divisions compose a *corps d'armée*, commanded by a major-general, or a lieutenant-general.

FORMATION OF A COMPANY.

The company being assembled on its ground, the sergeants, by the command *Fall in !* cause the rank and file (corporals and privates) to form in one rank, faced to the *right*, and in the order of height from right to left, (head of the rank to the foot;) the tallest man on the right, (now head of the rank,) the next tallest immediately covering the first, and so on to the left, or rear of the rank.

The first sergeant then gives the word

Front—FACE ! At the word FACE ! the company faces to the front, and the second sergeant places himself on the left of the rank.

The order is then given to *count off*.

The men then count off from the right, as *one two;* the third man counts *one* again and the fourth man *two*, and so on to the left of the rank.

The number two men compose the rear rank, and number ones the front rank.

In two ranks form company ! At this command number twos will take one step to the rear, number ones standing fast.

Close—RANKS! At the word RANKS! the men close together. Number *two* are then ordered to take one step to the right, which they do by stepping directly behind number one, leaving a space of thirteen inches between their breast and the back of the man in advance. Thus we have the company formed. The captain now divides the company into two equal parts. The first, composing the largest men, is called the *first platoon*, and the next, with the smallest men, the *second platoon.*

Each platoon is afterwards divided into two equal sections. They are numbered from right to left : *first, second, third,* and *fourth* section. The corporals (four in number) are then placed on the right and left of each platoon, in the front rank, according to height.

Between each platoon sufficient space should be allowed for wheeling to the right or left.

The officers and sergeants now take their posts as follows :—

The captain in the front rank, on the right of the company, his left elbow slightly touching the right of the front rank man.

The first lieutenant, two paces in rear of the rear rank and equi-distant between the centre of the second platoon and the second file from the left of the company.

The second lieutenant opposite the centre of the second platoon, and two paces in rear of the rear rank.

The first sergeant, on the right of the rear rank, covering the captain; he is denominated *covering sergeant*, or *right guide* of the company. The second sergeant, two paces in rear of the second file from the left of the company; he is denominated the *left guide* of the company. In the left company of a battalion, this sergeant, is on the left of the front rank; he is designated as the *closing sergeant*, and the corporal, the *covering corporal.*

The third sergeant, two paces in rear of the second file from the left of the first platoon.

The fourth sergeant, two paces in rear of the second file from the right of the second platoon.

The fifth sergeant, two paces in rear of the rear rank, and equi-distant between the second lieutenant and the third sergeant.

The pioneer is posted in the line of file-closers on the right; and the music in a line with the front rank, four paces on its right; the drummer on the right of the fifer or bugler. Absent officers and sergeants may be replaced, officers by sergeants, and sergeants by corporals, according to rank and the necessity of the case.

TO PASS FROM TWO RANKS INTO ONE RANK.

The order is given, *In one rank form company!* The left guide faces to the left.

MARCH! The left guide steps off and marches in the prolongation of the front rank; the next file steps off at the same time with the guide; the front rank man turns to the left at the first step, follows the guide, and is himself followed by the rear rank man of his file, who turns on the spot where his file-leader turned. The second file, counting from the left, and successively all the other files, march as prescribed for the first; the front rank man of each immediately following the rear rank man of the file next on the left. The captain *halts* the company as the last man on the right turns into the rank. The file-closers extend themselves with the movement.

IN COLUMN BY COMPANY.

The captain is two paces in front of the centre of his command; the first sergeant on the right of the front rank, and is the right guide of the company; the second sergeant on the left of the same rank, and is the left guide of the company.

IN COLUMN BY PLATOON.

The captain commands the first platoon, the first lieutenant the second platoon; each takes post two paces in front of the centre of his platoon; the first sergeant is the guide of the first platoon, and the second sergeant is the guide of the second platoon. They are on the left of the front rank of their respective platoons, if the column be right in front; and on the right (the company is reversed) if the left be in front.

If the column be marching in the route step, the chiefs of platoon take the place of the guides on the directing flank, and are covered by the latter in the rear rank.

IN COLUMN BY SECTION.

This column takes place only in column of route, and then only when platoons have a front of ten or more files. The captain commands the first section, the first lieutenant the third, the second lieutenant the second, and the third lieutenant the fourth section;—each taking post on the directing flank in the front rank of his section; the two guides who are thus displaced, each falls back to the rear rank of his section, and covers its chief; the remaining file-closers place themselves in the rear rank of their respective sections, all on the side of direction.

In column, except in column by sections, the file-closers, not otherwise provided for, are in their proper places behind the rear rank of their respective subdivisions.

In close column, or in column at half distance, they close up to within one pace of the rear rank. In column right in front, the left flank is the directing flank, (except under peculiar circumstances or manœuvres.) The reverse is the case in column left in front.

TO OPEN RANKS.

The company being at shoulder arms, the left guide is placed on the left of the rear rank.

To the rear—Open order!—At the word of command, the covering sergeant and the left guide step off to the rear, in the back step, four paces, and allign themselves parallel to the rear rank.

MARCH!—The front rank stands fast; the rear steps off in the back step, in common time, without counting steps, placing itself on the allignment marked out for it, and is alligned by the right on the left guide, by the covering sergeant. The file-closers step off at the same time with the rear rank, and place themselves two paces in the rear of that rank.

The ranks being properly alligned, the command *Front!* is given.

ALLIGNMENTS IN OPEN RANKS.

The ranks are first alligned man by man, as in the squad drill, three men being placed three paces in advance of the right or left of each rank, to serve as a basis, and the command given, *By file right* (or left)— *Dress!*—The men of each rank move up successively on the allignment, each man being preceded two paces by his neighbor. The ranks are next alligned at once, forward and backward, in both parallel and oblique directions, by the commands *right* (or left) *dress!* or *right* (or left) *backward dress!* three men, in each case, being placed on a basis. Before closing the ranks, the company should be exercised in the manual of arms, and the loadings in nine and four times and at will.

TO CLOSE RANKS.

Close order—MARCH!—At the command MARCH! the rear rank closes to the front, the men in the rear rank stepping briskly up, and covering his file-leader.

The company should next be instructed in the allignments and the manual of arms in closed ranks, and then proceed to the loadings and firings.

TO FIRE BY COMPANY.

Fire by company!—At this command the captain places himself opposite to the centre of his company, four paces in rear of the rank of file-closers. The covering sergeant places himself in that rank, opposite to his interval.

This rule is general for the captain and covering sergeant in all the different firings.

Commence—Firing!—At this command, the captain gives the words *company—ready—aim—fire—load!* At the word *load,* each man brings back his piece, loads, and comes to a shoulder, when the captain recommences the fire by the same commands, and thus continues it till orders to *cease firing*, (or the roll of the drum,) from his superior, (say colonel, if the company is attached to a regiment, and is drawn up in line of battle.)

The captain may sometimes cause aim to be taken to the right and left, by giving the words *right* (or left) *oblique* between the words *ready* and *aim*.

TO FIRE BY FILE.

Fire by file—Company—Ready—Commence—Firing— At the words *Commence Firing !* the right file aims and fires, and the next file aims at the instant the first has fired, and so on successively. After the first fire every man loads and fires without waiting for the others. (Fire at will.) Each man faces to the front in casting about, and after returning rammer springs up his piece with his left hand, and at the height of his chin, and makes a half face to the right, taking the position of *Ready*.

TO FIRE BY THE REAR RANK.

Face by the rear rank !—At this command the captain steps out and places himself near to, and facing the right file of the company ; the covering sergeant and file-closers pass quickly through the captain's interval, and place themselves faced to the rear, the covering sargeant a pace behind the captain, and the file-closers two paces from the front rank, opposite to their places in line.

Company about—face !—At the word *face !* given the

instant the last file-closer has passed through the interval, the company faces about; the captain places himself in the interval in the rear rank, (now front,) and the covering sergeant covers him in the front rank, (now rear.) The different firings are now executed in the manner already prescribed.

TO RESUME THE PROPER RANK.

Face by the front rank !—This is executed as prescribed in the command, *face by the rear rank—Company—About* —FACE!   The company having faced about, the captain and covering sergeant resume their places in line.

FORMATION OF A REGIMENT IN ORDER OF BATTLE.

The regiment is supposed to consist of ten companies, to wit : one grenadier company, one of light infantry or rifles, and eight battalion companies. Since the introduction of the famous zouave movements under the French military system, and the application of modern appliances of warfare, nearly all our volunteer regiments organize as rifle, or light infantry regiments, instead of as heavy infantry of the line. Opinions of military men differ, however, as to which is the most effective in actual combat. In our opinion, heavy infantry of the line belongs more properly to a past age, and could scarcely be near as efficient as a zouave or rifle regiment, well skilled in the sabre bayonet exercise, and the tactics so recently adopted by the French and United States governments.   The modern system seems to meet with more favor, as it certainly should among our citizen-soldiers. It affords quicker movements and combinations being made on the field, and therefore is not only really more serviceable in time of action, but less liable to loss by frequent shelling from rifled cannon in position at long range, than dense masses and slow-moving bodies of heavy infantry of the line.   The latter may repel a charge as well ; but in making a charge, or assaulting an intrenched position, the palm of superiority must be awarded to the former.

A regiment in order of battle is posted from right to left, as follows : first company, sixth, fourth, ninth, third, eighth, fifth, tenth, seventh and second, according to the rank of captains.

With a less number of companies, the same principle will be observed, viz. : the first captain assigned the command of the right company, the second captain the extreme left company of the regiment, the third captain the right centre company, and so on till the command is full.   The companies thus posted are designated from right to left—*first* company, *second* company, and so on to the ten companies.   The regimental colors should be posted on the left of the right centre battalion company. The five companies to the right of it are called the *right wing* of the battalion, and the five companies to the left the *left wing.*

The *color-bearer* should be a sergeant selected by the colonel, with two ranking corporals on his right and left.

The guard is composed of six corporals in addition. There should be no display of colors in battalions of less than five companies, and no color guard, except it may be at the reviews.

There are two *general guides* to each battalion, selected from among the second or third sergeants by the colonel. The first one is called the *right general guide*, posted in rear of the right flank of the battalion, and the second the *left general guide* posted in the line of file-closers, in rear of the left flank of the battalion. The field music is posted twelve paces in rear of left centre company, and band five paces in rear of the field music.

FIELD OFFICERS AND REGIMENTAL STAFF.

The field officers, colonel, lieutenant-colonel, and major should be mounted on horseback. The adjutant, when the battalion is manœuvring, will be on foot.

The colonel's post is thirty paces in the rear, and opposite the centre of the battalion.

The lieutenant-colonel twelve paces in the rear, and opposite the centre of the right wing.

The major twelve paces in the rear, and opposite the centre of the left wing.

The adjutants and sergeant-major opposite the right and left of the battalion, respectively, and eight paces in the rear of the file-closers.

The quartermaster, surgeon, and other staff officers, in one rank, on the left of the colonel and three paces in his rear.

The quartermaster-sergeant, on a line with the front rank of the field music, and two paces on the right.

The adjutant and sergeant-major will aid the colonel and major in the manœuvres.

In the absence of the colonel, then the lieutenant-colonel will take command. In his absence, the major, and in the major's absence then the senior captain.

OFFICERS AND NON-COMMISSIONED OFFICERS.

Officers and non-commissioned officers are in the following rank :

1. Lieutenant-general,
2. Major-general,
3. Brigade-general,
4. Colonel,
5. Lieutenant-colonel,
6. Major,
7. Captain,
8. First Lieutenant,
9. Second Lieutenant,
10. Ensign,
11. Sergeant-major,
12. Quartermaster—sergeant of a regiment,
13. Ordnance—sergeant, and Hospital Steward,
14. First Sergeant,
15. Sergeant,
16. Corporal.

Each grade takes precedence in rank by date of commission, or appointment. Brevet rank is a mere honorary distinction, and does not give precedence.

Officers commissioned by any State take rank next *after* officers of like grade commissioned by the Federal Government.

Resignations will not take effect until information of their acceptance is made known.

PRINCIPLES OF SHOULDERED ARMS.

The piece in the right hand, the barrel resting in the hollow of the shoulder, the guard to the front, the arm bent slightly, and hanging easy near the body, the thumb and fore-finger embracing the guard, the remaining fingers closed together and grasping the swell of the stock, directly under the cock, which rests on the little finger.

Care will be taken that the piece be not carried too high or too low ; the right elbow in the rank should be close to the body, and sufficient space allowed the soldier to handle his piece with facility.

Support—ARMS !

(First motion.)—Bring the piece with the right hand to the front, perpendicularly between the eyes, the barrel to the rear ; seize the piece with the left hand at the lower band, raise this hand as high as the chin, and seize the piece at the same time with the right hand four inches below the cock.

(Second motion.)—Turn the piece with the right hand, the barrel to the front ; carry the piece to the left shoulder, and pass the fore-arm, extended on the breast, between the right hand and the cock ; support the cock against the left fore-arm, and then rest the left hand on the right breast.

(Third motion.)—Drop the right hand by the side.

REST !

At this word, bring up quickly the right hand to the handle of the piece, (small of the stock.)

When this position is assumed, it will not be required to preserve silence, or steadiness of position.

When the instructor may wish the recruit to pass from this position to that of steadiness he will command

Attention—SQUAD, (or COMPANY!)

At the second word, the recruit will drop the right hand to the side, and maintain silence in the rank.

Shoulder—ARMS !

One time and three motions.

(First motion.)—Grasp the piece with the right hand under and against the left fore-arm; seize it with the left hand at the lower band, the thumb extended; detach the piece slightly from the shoulder, the left fore-arm along the stock.

(Second motion.)—Carry the piece vertically to the right shoulder with both hands, the rammer to the front; change the position of the right hand so as to embrace the guard with the thumb and fore-finger, slip the left hand to the height of the shoulder, the fingers extended and joined, the right arm nearly straight.

(Third motion.)—Drop the left hand quickly by the side.

Present—ARMS!

One time and two motions.

(First motion.)—With the right hand bring the piece erect before the centre of the body, rammer to the front; at the same time seize the piece with the left hand half-way between the guide-sight and lower band, the thumb extended along the barrel, and against the stock, the fore-arm horizontal, and resting against the body, the hand as high as the elbow.

(Second motion.)—Grasp the small of the stock with the right hand below and against the guard.

Shoulder—ARMS!

One time and two motions.

(1.) Bring the piece to the right shoulder, at the same time change the position of the right hand so as to embrace the guard with the thumb and forefinger; slip the left hand to the height of the shoulder, the fingers extended and joined, the right arm nearly straight.

(2.) Drop the left hand quickly by the side.

Order—ARMS!

One time and two motions.

(1.) Seize the piece promptly at the word *Order!* with the left hand near the upper band, and detach it slightly from the shoulder with the right hand; loosen the right hand, lower the piece with the left; re-seize the piece with the right hand above the lower band, the little finger in rear of the barrel, the butt about four inches from the round, the right hand supported against the hip; drop the left hand by the side.

(2.) Let the piece slip through the right hand, by opening slightly the fingers, to the ground. The hand low, the barrel between the thumb and forefinger, extending along the stock; the other fingers extended and joined; the muzzle about two inches from the right shoulder; the rammer in front; the toe (or beak) of the butt against and in a line with the toe of the right foot; the barrel perpendicular.

REST!

At this command, assume an easy position, standing of course in the rank.

Attention—SQUAD, (or COMPANY!)

At the second word, resume the position of order arms.

Shoulder—ARMS!

One time and two motions.

(1.) Raise the piece vertically with the right hand to the height of the right breast, opposite shoulder; elbow close to the body; seize the piece with left hand, below the right, and drop quickly the right hand to grasp the swell of the stock, the thumb and forefinger embracing the guard; press the piece against the shoulder with the left hand; the right arm nearly straight.

(2.) Drop left hand quickly by the side.

Load in nine times—

LOAD!

Grasp the piece with the left hand, as high as right elbow; bring it vertically opposite middle of the body; shift the right hand to the upper band; place the butt between the feet, the barrel to the front; seize it with left hand near the muzzle, which should be three inches from the body; carry the right hand to the cartridge-box.

Handle—CARTRIDGE!

Seize cartridge with thumb and two fingers, and place it between the teeth.

Tear—CARTRIDGE!

Bite the end of the paper to the powder; hold the cartridge upright, and in this position place it in front, and near the muzzle; keep the back of the hand to the front.

Charge—CARTRIDGE!

Empty the powder quickly into the barrel; disengage the ball from the paper with the right hand and the thumb, and first two fingers of the left; insert it in the bore, the pointed end uppermost, and press it down with the right thumb; seize the head of the rammer with the thumb and forefinger of the right hand; the other fingers closed, and elbows near the body.

Draw—RAMMER!

Half draw the rammer by extending the right arm; steady it in this position with the left thumb; grasp the rammer with the right hand near the muzzle, the little finger uppermost, the nails to the front, the thumb extended along the rammer.

Clear the rammer by drawing it forth; turn the rammer, the little end passing near the left shoulder; place the head of it on the ball, the back of the hand to the front.

Ram—CARTRIDGE!

Insert the rammer, and press the ball home.

Return—RAMMER!

Draw the rammer half way out with the right hand, and steady it in this position with the left thumb; run the right hand down the rammer again to the muzzle; extend the arm, turn the rammer, the head near the left shoulder; steady it in its "pipes" with the left thumb and forefinger, and force it home; at the same instant, passing the left hand down the barrel to the extent of the arm, and steady your piece without depressing the shoulder.

PRIME!

One time and two motions.

(1.) With the left hand raise the piece till the hand is as high as the eye; grasp the small of the stock with the right hand; half face to the right, at the same time place the hollow of the right foot within an inch of the left heel; slip the left hand down to the lower band, the thumb along the stock; left elbow against the body; bring the piece to the right side, the butt below the right forearm, the small of the stock against the body, and two inches below the right breast, the barrel upwards, and the muzzle on a level with the right eye.

(2.) Cock your piece with the thumb; then take a cap from the pouch, place it on the nipple, and press it down with the thumb; after which seize the small of the stock with the right hand.

Shoulder—Arms!

(1.) Bring piece to right shoulder, and support it with left hand.

(2.) Drop left hand quickly to the side.

Ready!

Bring the butt to the right shoulder, and lower the muzzle of the piece with both hands; cock and seize the piece at the small of the stock with the right hand, the left extending along the barrel; the muzzle as high as the eye.

Keep the right thumb on the head of the cock, and the other fingers under and against the guard.

Aim!

Cast your eye along the sight of the piece to the object aimed at; carry the right foot twelve inches to the right, and towards the left heel of the man next on the right, inclining the upper part of the body forward; keep the right elbow on a line with the shoulder.

8

FIRE!

Press the forefinger of the right hand against the trigger, and fire without lowering or turning the head, and remain in this position.   If, after the firing, the instructor should not wish the recruits to reload, he will order shoulder arms.

Recover—ARMS !

To accustom the recruit to wait for the command *fire !* after the order is given to aim, the instructor should command *recover—arms !*   At the first part of the command withdraw the finger from the trigger; at the command *arms !* assume the position of *ready.*

The recruit should be frequently practised in the manœuvre to *aim* and then *recover arms,* to familiarize him with the word of command.

Secure—ARMS !

(1.) Bring the piece with the right hand to the front, perpendicularly to the front, and between the eyes, the barrel to the rear ; seize the piece with the left hand at the lower band, raise this hand as high as the chin, and seize the piece with the right hand at the small of the stock.

(2.) Turn the piece with both hands, the barrel to the front ; bring it opposite the left shoulder, the butt against the hip, the left hand at the lower band, the thumb as high as the chin, and extended on the rammer ; the piece erect and detached from the shoulder, the left forearm against the piece.

(3.) Reverse the piece, pass it under the left arm, the left hand remaining at the lower band, the thumb on the rammer, to prevent it from sliding out, the little finger resting against the hip, the right hand falling at the same time by the side.

Arms—AT WILL !

Carry the piece at pleasure, on either shoulder, with one or both hands, the muzzle always up.

Arms—PORT!

Throw the piece diagonally across the body, the lock to the front, seize it smartly, at the same instant, with both hands, the right at the handle, the left at the tail band, the two thumbs pointing towards the muzzle, the barrel sloping upwards and crossing opposite to the point of the left shoulder, the butt proportionally lowered. The palm of the right hand above that of the left, under the piece, and the nails of both next to the body, to which the elbows are closed.

Carry—ARMS!

(1.) Carry quickly the right hand to the small.

(2.) Place quickly the left hand on the butt.

(3.) Let fall smartly the right hand into its position, and drop with the left, at the same time, the piece into the position of shoulder arms.

Right Shoulder Shift!

(1.) Supposing the recruit was at a shoulder arms: Detach the piece perpendicularly with the right hand, and seize it with the left between the lower band and guide-sight, raise the piece, the left hand at the height of the shoulder and four inches from it; place at the same time the right hand on the butt, the beak between the first two fingers, the other two fingers under the butt plate.

(2.) Quit the piece with the left hand, raise and place the piece on the right shoulder with the right hand, the lock plate upwards.

Let fall, at the same time, the left hand by the side.

Ground—Arms!

(1.) From a shoulder arms.—Turn the piece with the right hand, the barrel to the left; at the same time seize the cartridge-box with the left hand, bend the body, advance the left foot, the heel opposite the lower band, the knees slightly bent, and lay the piece on the ground with the right hand.

(2.) Rise up, and bring the feet together, and drop the hands by the side.

Raise—Arms!

(1.) Seize the cartridge-box with the left hand, bend the body, advance the left foot opposite the lower band, and seize the piece with the right hand.

(2.) Raise the piece, bring the feet together, turn the piece with the right hand, the rammer to the front, at the same time drop the left hand by the side.

Fix—BAYONET!

From a shoulder arms.

(1.) Grasp the piece with the left hand at the height of the shoulder.

(2.) Quit the piece with the right hand, lower it with the left hand opposite the middle of the body, and place the butt between the feet, the rammer to the rear, the barrel vertical, the muzzle three inches from the body; seize it with the right hand at the upper band, and carry the left hand to the bayonet.

(3.) Draw the bayonet, and fix it on the end of the barrel, seize the piece with the left hand, the arm extended, the right hand at the upper band; come to a shoulder arms.

Charge—BAYONET!

(1.) Raise the piece slightly with the right hand, and make a half face to the right, place the hollow of the right foot opposite to, and three inches from the left heel, the feet square, seize the piece at the same time with the left hand a little above the lower band.

(2.) Bring down the piece with both hands, the barrel uppermost, the left elbow against the body; seize the small of the stock at the same time with the right hand, which will be supported against the hip, the point of the bayonet as high as the eye.

Trail—ARMS!

From a shoulder arms.

(1.) The same as the first motion of order arms.

(2.) Incline the muzzle slightly to the front, the butt to the rear, and about four inches from the ground. The right hand, supported at the hip, will so hold the piece that the rear rank men may not touch, with their bayonets, the men in the front rank.

Unfix—BAYONET!

From a shoulder arms.

(First and second motions.) The same as the first and second motions to fix bayonet, except that the thumb of the right hand will be pressed on the spring, if a sabre bayonet, and with the same hand wrest the bayonet off the edge (or point) to the front, and return it to its scabbard, and seize the piece with the left hand, the arm extended. The next movement, shoulder arms.

To *Stack*—ARMS.

The squad being in two ranks at order arms.

Stack—ARMS!—At the command, the front rank man of every even-numbered file passes his piece before him, seizing it with the left hand above the middle band, and places the butt behind and near the right foot of the man next on the left, the barrel turned to the front. At the same time the front rank man of every odd-numbered file passes his piece before him, seizing it with the left hand below the middle band, and hands it to the man next on the left; the latter receives it with the right hand two inches above the middle band, throws the butt about thirty-two inches to the front, opposite to his right shoulder, inclining the muzzle towards him, and locks the shanks of the two bayonets, the lock of this second piece towards the right, and its shank above that of the first piece.

The rear rank man of every even file projects his bayonet forward, and introduces it (using both hands) between and *under* the shanks of the two other bayonets. He then abandons his piece to his file-leader, who receives it with the right hand under the middle band, brings the butt to the front, holding up his own piece and the stack with the left hand, and places the butt of this third piece between the feet of the man next on the right.

The stack thus formed, the rear rank man of every odd file passes his piece into his left hand, the barrel turned to the front, and sloping the bayonet forward rests it on the stack.

Break—RANKS!

To dispose of the command, the order is given to—
Break ranks—MARCH!

To resume—ARMS !

The squad, on a signal, or order to fall in, re-forms in two ranks.

The next order is to resume arms, when each man advances and seizes his piece.

When companies stack arms, the sergeants, and also corporals, if in the rank of file-closers, rest their pieces against the stacks nearest to them, respectively, *after* ranks are broken, and resume their pieces on the signal to re-form ranks.

The color-guard forms a separate stack.

LOAD AND FIRE AT WILL!

When the command is given to load and fire at will, each recruit will load and fire with care, but at the same time with celerity and despatch. Much depends on beating an enemy to load and fire two or three times if possible to his once. The recruit, therefore, should learn to handle his piece with ease and dexterity.

MARCHING AND WHEELING MOVEMENTS.

With the limited space at command, it would be impossible to give full and complete directions of the marching and wheeling movements at present in vogue in the Army of the United States. A competent drill-master can more readily instruct a body of recruits in evolutions and manœuvres than for them to endeavor to learn the various movements from long written descriptions, and series of illustrated plates.

We must content ourselves, therefore, in giving the commands only which it is absolutely necessary for a recruit to perfect himself in to become a good soldier, without going into extended details. They are to—

Mark time—March.

Forward—March.

To change step.

To march backwards.

To march to the front.

Right oblique.

Left oblique.

To march to the front in double-quick time.

Quick time.

To face about in marching.

Squad right about.

The march by the flank.

By file left (or right)—March.

To march by the flank in double-quick time.

Wheeling from a halt, or on a fixed pivot.

Wheeling and changing direction to the side of the guide, in double-quick time.

Long marches in double-quick time, and the run.

To open ranks.

Allignments in open ranks.

To close ranks.

To march in line of battle.

To halt the company marching in line of battle, and to allign it.

Oblique march in line of battle.

To march in double-quick time, and the back step.

To march in retreat in line of battle.

To change direction by file.

To halt the company marching by the flank and to face it to the front.

In march by the flank to form company, on the right or left by fire into line of battle.

To break into column by platoon, either at a halt, or while marching.

To march in column.

To change direction.

Being in column by platoons, to form to the right or left into line of battle, either at a halt or marching.

To break into platoons and to re-form the company.

To break files to the rear and to cause them to re-enter into line.

To march in column *en route*, and to execute the movements incident thereto.

Countermarch.

To advance in line of battle.

Being in column to break files to the rear, and to cause them to re-enter into line.

Break into sections.

Form platoons.

INSTRUCTIONS FOR SKIRMISHERS.

To deploy forward.

To deploy by the flank.

To extend intervals.

To close intervals.

To relieve skirmishers.

To advance in line.

To retreat in line.

To change direction.

To march by the flank.

To fire at a halt.

To fire marching.

The rally, by sections, by platoons, and on the reserve.

To form column to march in any direction.

The assembly.

GENERAL CALLS FOR BUGLER AND DRUM-MAJOR.

1. Attention.
2. The general.
3. The assembly.
4. To the color.
5. The recall.
6. Quick time.
7. Double-quick time.
8. The charge.
9. The reveille. — WAKE UP
10. Retreat.
11. Tattoo. — LIGHTS OUT
12. To extinguish lights.
13. Assembly of the buglers.
14. Assembly of the guard.
15. Orders for orderly sergeants.
16. For officers to take their places in line after firing.
17. The disperse.
18. Officers' call.
19. Breakfast call.
20. Dinner call.
21. Sick call
22. Fatigue call.
23. Church call.
24. Drill call.
25. School call.

CALLS FOR SKIRMISHERS.

1. Fix bayonet.
2. Unfix bayonet.
3. Quick time.
4. Double-quick time.
5. The run.
6. Deploy as skirmishers.
7. Forward.
8. In retreat.
9. Halt.
10. By the right flank.
11. By the left flank.
12. Commence firing.
13. Cease firing.
14. Change direction to the right.
15. Change direction to the left.
16. Lie down.
17. Rise up.
18. Rally by fours.
19. Rally by sections.
20. Rally by platoons.
21. Rally on the reserve.
22. Rally on the battalion.
23. Assemble on the battalion.

Check Out More Titles From HardPress Classics Series In this collection we are offering thousands of classic and hard to find books. This series spans a vast array of subjects – so you are bound to find something of interest to enjoy reading and learning about.

Subjects:
Architecture
Art
Biography & Autobiography
Body, Mind &Spirit
Children & Young Adult
Dramas
Education
Fiction
History
Language Arts & Disciplines
Law
Literary Collections
Music
Poetry
Psychology
Science
…and many more.

Visit us at www.hardpress.net

WS - #0233 - 130723 - C0 - 229/152/9 - PB - 9781318687701 - Gloss Lamination